AF426576

Praise for Studio of the Voice

Essaying is the best way to freeze and examine and better understand the shifting phantasmagoria of our experiences in families and societies, and Marcia Aldrich's *Studio of the Voice* is a whole collection of essays par excellence. With an eager, associative mind, Aldrich gathers and explores intergenerational conflicts and conundrums, generating meditative momentum toward a new vision of how we should, and can, relate to one another.

—Patrick Madden, author of *Disparates: Essays*

In *Studio of the Voice*, Marcia Aldrich creates a studio of the voice-driven essay. Endlessly curious, digressive, formally inventive, these essays shine a light on an essential quality of the essay: it's not about the epiphany, but process, the questions one asks. Long one of our very best essayists, Aldrich is undaunted at the dark door of the multifaceted truths self-investigation can yield, though sometimes, surprisingly, it is only the door that is dark. One essay by Marcia Aldrich is a cause for celebration. This rangy new book should provoke a parade. A signal achievement, *Studio of the Voice* is an essential book of essays.

—David Lazar, author of *Celeste Holm Syndrome*
and founding editor of *Hotel Amerika*

No writer evokes the way Marcia Aldrich evokes. For every scene she writes, story she tells, detail she describes, she palpates the imagination. This book is physicality incarnate. I can feel her hands as they clutch a bedpost, soothe a cheek slap, twist the chain of a pair of smudged reading glasses hanging around the neck, warm with a flash of menopause, rub the arch of Marilyn Monroe's foot, burnish beauty, weigh the heaviness of rejection, thrill at the joy of a backflip, and press through dark water with the joy of swimming. *Studio of the Voice* maintains that we are most human when we are most embodied. Aldrich makes us feel fully human as she gives voice to her own body and the bodies of others in this vibrantly corporeal book.

—Nicole Walker, author of *Processed Meat:
Essays on Food, Flesh, and Navigating Disaster*

Studio of the Voice is a polyphonic study in the nature of voice. Like the best essayists, Marcia Aldrich asks tough questions and explores a multitude of possible answers. Some questions lead to new ways of seeing, whether a fresh perspective on a famed portrait of Marilyn Monroe and her fascinating feet, or Jane Fonda's character in the film *Klute*, or her own mother's thick curling toenails. Other questions lead to self-reckoning, taking the measure of the self's many roles: daughter, mother, young woman, middle-aged woman, lover, wife, swimmer, professor, writer.

Under Aldrich's piercing gaze, the voice can be the spoken word, sometimes quiet and stifled, sometimes surprising and provocative--as when she tells male academic colleagues her career has been unlike theirs because of sex. Or the voice can be the written word, carefully crafted in experimental form (abecedarian, diagram, second person) or in classic questioning essay mode. Often, the body becomes a kind of voice, powerful in a fitted blue dress when a broken-down New York City apartment and isolating job at a law firm stifle almost every other aspect of voice. Or when swimming in competition, or refusing to strike a pose that will produce a photograph that says "writer." Sometimes the body slips into a sidestroke, and the writer in a sense becomes her mother, who favored that paradoxical stroke, weak and disqualified from competition, yet lifesaving in preserving energy and allowing a drowning person to be carried ashore.

The book probes the spaces of intimacy—the marital bed, the separate beds of the parents, labor pains and birth, a post-menopausal gynecological exam, sex and seduction—marrying and divorcing her college professor, then marrying for life. The book probes the big questions—why she has no birth story, the challenges of balancing writing, academia, and motherhood, grief and longing.

In every section, every individual essay, you will find a voice that dazzles, soars, flies, swims, sings.

—Jocelyn Bartkevicius, author of "How to Survive in Lithuania" and former editor of *Florida Review*

STUDIO of the VOICE

essays by Marcia Aldrich

Wandering Aengus Press
wanderingaenguspress.com

First Edition. Published by Wandering Aengus Press

Nonfiction
ISBN: 979-8-218-20486-0
Cover Photo: Matthias Boeckel, Pixabay
Book Design: Jill McCabe Johnson
Author Photo: Kathleen Atkins

Wandering Aengus Press
PO Box 334 Eastsound, WA 98245
wanderingaenguspress.com

Wandering Aengus Press is dedicated to publishing works to enrich lives and make the world a better place.

Contents

To my many mothers

THE STRONGER ONE

The Mother Bed

For my mother's first wedding her father commissioned a maple bedroom suite: an armoire, a dresser, and twin beds, all in a French country style, with graceful lines like the lift and fall of willows and resting on carved claw-feet. Twin beds were not a common choice for the bridal chamber, and I have always supposed that by splitting the conjugal bed in two, my grandfather—whose own marriage had been riven by a precipitous divorce when my mother was just a little girl—was saying something sly about matrimony. Such was his wit and the rough joinery of his heart. In receiving this burdened gift my mother accepted more than some items of handsome property (or so it would be were I writing a novel), for her own marriage also ended abruptly when, having borne two daughters in quick succession, she was widowed by the mining fire that killed her husband, Tommy. For the next five years she slept in one of the beds while its mate, perfectly composed, lay empty, or rather, gave repose to a ghost. My mother then met and wed my father, and the maple bedroom suite came with her into what is fairly called a posthumous married life.

    Thus it was that through all the nights of their marriage, my mother slept in *her* bed, and my father slept in *his*. But why did my father accept this arrangement, this division between husband and wife? Why did he agree to sleep in a bed made for another man, take his rest, his sojourn in dreams, on a laden reminder of his wife's lost life, and look morning and night on a freighted decor? Why did he not insist that the twin beds be replaced with a new king or queen? There were practical reasons not to do so, of course, for the willow beds were beautiful and well built, and to get rid of them and buy their like would have been expensive. However, cost cannot have counted for so much in the reckoning, for my parents were always ready to spend on new drapes and sofas that took the place of what were, to my eye, perfectly good drapes and sofas. No, they could have replaced the two beds with one, and would have, as they replaced all the other furniture in the house, were it not for some potent obstacle: It was my mother who would not part with the beds and build anew. She said, in effect, let no man join what God hath put asunder. She insisted my father accept love-laden, lovelorn furniture from a former marriage, and he, remarkably, did so.

My father's acquiescence to the beds was possible, I believe, only as one clause in a larger agreement, an overarching marital strategy that was acutely practiced in the bedroom but applied more widely. You could call it hiding in plain sight. My father accepted the beds so long as no one talked about them or whence they came. Spend intimate hours nightly on the beds but do not speak of their provenance—that was the deal. Here we come to a point that is, for obvious reasons, of special concern to me. For out of this silent deal, *I* was born, and out of it grew my child's sense of a self in a family. It was this deal, this tension, this bridge held up by counterpoised tensions, this incongruity of the obvious and the unspoken, the fact and the denial of the fact—not just with the beds but with all of my mother's first marital experience—that created for me the child a secretive mystery to my family's hidden past. And since in my formative years the evidence was there before me in plain sight daily, and yet silently denied by all, and since this strategy applied not just to my family's past but to my family's present, this bargain of oblivion created a secretiveness and mysteriousness that suffused my whole child life.

As for my father's feelings, he could not simply acquiesce to the bedroom decor and lie quietly, deal or no deal. That is not the modus operandi of human emotions, and you don't need a master of feng shui to explain it. In such a bedroom, tensions arise that must be diffused or contained. Emotional costs erased on one ledger show up on another balance sheet. Sleeping in the willow bed did not solve the problem that dwelled in it, no matter how many nights my father spent there, not a thousand nights, not ten thousand nights and more. In my family, emotions are more durable than that. Their shelf life is basically forever. Ancient hurts thought to be forever buried in permafrost can emerge intact, like a woolly mammoth out of a melting glacier.

Sleeping in separate beds, my parents neither retired at the same time nor awoke together. It was as if a tectonic shift had forced them together from different time zones. On workdays my father rose early and headed to the coffee shop for breakfast, leaving his bed unmade. There during the night he had waged a battle of heroic proportions against an unknown foe. The sheets had come unmoored from the mattress and been tossed so insistently as to become knotted. The blankets and bedcover were whipped and heaved into stiff peaks at the foot of the bed, while at the head his pillow looked punch drunk. As he dressed to go to work, atop the mix he tossed his limp pajamas, white with blue piping like the sheets. My mother's bed, meanwhile, was intact, even as she lay in it. All was tucked in, untrammeled, smooth. If I got up early on Saturday, I could find a languid body there that did not move—my long, thin mother, sleeping on her side, head hardly dusting the pillow, as if she were a weightless flower, perhaps a stargazer. Slippers lay at the side of her bed like tiny obedient dogs, and when my mother began her day, she first put on her slippers and then painstakingly remade my father's bed.

As for retiring to bed together at night, they did not. This disjunction was well settled between them and was not a node of conflict, at least so far as I was aware. However, there was once a telltale scene of my father's trying to get them to bed together on a Saturday night. I had been left at home with a babysitter while my parents went out. When they returned, I was in the den down the hall from their bedroom, watching a movie, one of the tragic animal tales by means of which I liked to self-traumatize. Tipsy from the evening's festivities, my father dismissed the sitter, got ready for bed, and, calling from the bedroom, urged my mother to join him.

"Marge, come to bed," he called out, saying her name with a husky slur. I had never heard him say it in this way before. But instead of complying, my mother perched on the thin arm of a hard chair in the den, feigning interest in my movie. Never in her life had she stayed up to watch a movie with me. Never in my life had I been allowed to stay up and finish one. My father called out to her several times, first in rising tones, like a question, and then, as the minutes passed, sinking, with one last "Muhge." She balanced unsteadily on the chair arm, tense, as if warding off something distasteful, as I would if presented with a loathsome item of food, lima beans perhaps, or okra. When my father finally fell asleep and snored, my mother moved off into the bedroom and her single bed.

If I step back for a moment and view matters with a sociological eye, I see that my parents' marital bargain was related to but distinct from one commonly struck in their social circle, by which neither husband nor wife need grasp what occupied the other's time day to day. The wife knew next to nothing about the husband's professional life, and she, so long as dinner appeared when he came home hungry from work, so long as clean, pressed shirts hung in the closet, could go about her business as she wished. Though this much was true of my mother and father also, they differed from other couples who, despite separate daytime lives, retired to the same bed, as I observed each time I slept over at a friend's house. The dimensions of the bed varied from the modest double to the grandiose king, but whatever the frame, husband and wife fit themselves into it. My parents were in this respect known outliers, and their twin beds became something of a curiosity in *my* social circle. When friends spent the night at my house, we would tiptoe down the long hallway to the master bedroom and stand in the doorway, looking at the beds as if we were visiting mummies in the British Museum, perfectly wrapped in matching spreads of pale green satin. The two beds, in the spirit of the old movie code, were separated by a night table that, compact as it was, might as well have been Canada.

From my observations I drew unhappy conclusions about the state of my parents' marital enterprise—no, not conclusions, for my childish feelings were far more formless than that. I did not know what sex was—I knew or felt only that children came like Bambi from the vague association of male and female—and I was unable to deduce that my father must have crossed the chasm at least once, making the nocturnal journey from bed to bed and back again. And yet I *sensed* it, for otherwise I could not be, even while the distant beds bespoke a missing intimacy, emblematic of a whole arrangement. It seemed dimly to me a miracle or a mistake that I had been conceived at all, and this too was a part of the mystery of my green life, of myself as a child to my mother and father, and of my place in relation to my mother's past.

My mother never spoke of her first husband or the years immediately following his death, certainly not to me or in my presence. I was told of the marriage in a most cursory way when, at the age of six or seven, I asked why my sisters' last name differed from my own. No photographs of her first marriage were displayed in the house, nothing shown of the family group. There were two shots of my sisters as little girls, which sat in gilded frames side by side on my mother's dresser. Their upper bodies only—the rest of their persons having been cropped—were suspended against a backdrop of pink-and-blue sky. They had been touched up, their cheeks unnaturally rosy to match rosebud lips, eyes and hair darkened too precisely. Behind the photos of my sisters loomed an ornate mirror, part of the willow suite, which reflected my mother's bed. Across the room, on top of my father's taller dresser, sat a photograph of me perched on a grand piano. I wore a fancy dress, little white socks ruffled at the ankles, and shiny black patent leather shoes.

All of these observations, all of my suppositions and wonder and the silence, brewed in me a strong curiosity about my mother's past. Even to glimpse it, as on one occasion I was able to, was an epoch in my childhood. I was looking for a Halloween costume in the crawl space in the basement, and there I found a suitcase, the lid closed, the suitcase shoved out of sight into the dark bowels of the house.

I pulled the case out onto the cement floor where the light was better. Constructed as if to withstand natural disasters, it was reinforced with steel. The exterior had a hardened, waxy finish, almost glazed a grainy yellow, with wide bands of black cross-hatched on the top and bottom. The case was not locked, as I expected it to be. When I pressed the metal latches, they popped up as if new and freshly oiled.

Nothing prepared me for what I found inside: a tumble of images, thrown topsy-turvy into the case, of my mother in her former life, of my sisters as little girls in their father's arms, suspended in time before I was born, an armful of small, square snapshots depicting a happy family to which I did not belong. In one black-and-white photo my mother was holding my sister above her shoulders in a dappled sunlight. Mother and child smiled back and forth at one another, ready to break into giddy laughter for no reason but happiness with the moment. Photos of my mother's first wedding and honeymoon were tossed into the jumble, many of these more formal, taken by professionals. There was my mother's first husband, Tommy. Even in those few moments of looking, I saw that he was unlike my father. Perfect really, a perfectly beautiful young man. Husband and wife were lifted out of the bland frame of ordinary life and cast in the extraordinary glow of their tropical honeymoon, leaning toward one another under slender palms. Happiness radiated from my mother's lifted, expressive eyes.

The flood of images made my heart race. I felt as if I were a robber, breaking and entering my mother's memories, where I had never been invited. I half listened for her footsteps, afraid that her face, much more glum than the face in the photographs, might appear over my shoulder. There was so much to take in that I had never seen before, a home movie on fast forward, the frames speeding by like windows with silhouettes on a commuter train as it disappeared into a dark tunnel. Some of the photos were bent, discolored, piled together like the notes of a beautiful melody, scrambled and disordered. Yet they formed a story of romantic love and happiness, and they were not what I saw in my parents' marriage.

Soon my fear of being caught overcame my desire to look further, and I closed the suitcase and returned it to the crawl space. When days later I stole back for another peek, the suitcase was gone. I never saw it again. By some means my mother had learned that I had tampered with it. She must have visited the suitcase periodically, perhaps regularly, and on one of her visits discovered it had been opened. Did I not return it to its exact location? Were there signs of intrusion? She must have known that I was the one who had broken in. Why didn't she speak to me about it? We maintained a complete silence on the matter, as on so much else between us. I could never broach the subject, for it lay outside the carefully drawn lines of our relationship. I wondered what she did with the photos. Did she store the suitcase in some place so secret, so remote, so unassailable that no one would ever find it?

Inside the suitcase lived a mother and a woman entirely different from the mother and woman I knew. There resided a young mother with an easy smile who delighted in her young girls—carefree, soft, and vibrant. This, I felt, was my mother's true family, to which I did not belong. The true family was the one that gathered at my house at Christmas, my mother, my sisters, and Aunt Virgie, Uncle Bob, and Uncle Harry, Tommy's mother and brothers, who distinguished their own blood from mine, and brought lavish gifts for my sisters, and drab things for me, and who burdened the day, and made me an outsider in my own life.

The distance between my parents did not diminish as I grew up and left home, as my father retired; as they moved many times, passed into old age, and my mother declined into dementia.

In the final condominium, they occupied different bedrooms, each anchoring one end of their quarters and parted by a long hallway. My mother resided with the old bedroom suite, while my father slept on a new single cherrywood bed picked out by him at Ethan Allen. After a long marriage defined by separation, they found no relief from each other's company in the last years. My father was afraid to leave my mother alone, and she was afraid to be left. If he ran a brief errand, he could not be certain she would stay put inside. He might find her on the front walk in her nightgown, flailing her arms in fear, for she could not remember where her husband had gone, or when he might return.

Near the desperate end of my mother's life, my father sometimes phoned me in the afternoon when she was napping, for then he could speak freely. His muffled voice was shaken, and he would say that he no longer knew the woman he had married. There were depths of despair in her that he had not known existed. "She says terrible things," he told me, though he would not specify. Our conversations were brief, often cut short when my mother woke up from her nap. Even when she did not appear, my father sounded anxious, as if looking over his shoulder and hurrying because he did not have much time.

Then she died, from a brain hemorrhage caused by a fall. My husband and I drove down for the funeral, and after the service we accompanied my father back to his condominium to spend the night, wanting to provide some company as he began his solitude, though I did not know what to say, or how to help him. The pantry was empty, and the kitchen bare except for copies of the newspaper obituary that lay on the counter. A plant in pink foil, already beleaguered when I had visited a month before, was stuffed into a trash can whose lid would now not shut. I had brought back from the funeral an ornate floral bouquet, which I placed on the table in the dining room. There, stacked on the table by my father, were a dozen old-fashioned photo albums and ornately worked leather folders. In them, carefully arranged in storybook binders, was the lost cache of images from the yellow suitcase, chronicling my mother's first marriage. Her wedding and honeymoon were there, lovingly detailed in formal photographs, while informal shots preserved the short years of the family. It was their life as I had remembered it, blessed and happy. I was glad to learn that my mother had not eradicated the suitcase when she hid it from me forty years earlier. I felt, strange to say, a small triumph. The story of the suitcase and my mother's secret unhappiness was the one I had been telling myself for a long time, and the story had come true. But now a new mystery arose. Was my mother's unhappiness made endurable or deepened by visiting the suitcase?

As I looked at the albums and pondered, my father sat in his easy chair, staring at its sage-green mate. With an edge to his voice he said, "Take one or two binders if you'd like."

But I did not want any of the long-hidden photos. Even after my mother's death, they did not seem mine to take. I closed the album and joined my father in the living room. There was only her seat left, and reluctantly I took it, facing the window where the afternoon light failed during the minutes we sat silent. Then my father spoke, and bitterness poured out of him. In all the years of their marriage, he said, my mother had never spoken of her first husband, until dementia loosened her tongue, and out came his name.

"It was Tommy this and Tommy that," my father said. "She pushed me away, told me she couldn't bear me, had never been able to bear me." She told him Tommy had been her only true husband.

Now, I felt, I could finish the old story. It must have been that my mother's desire for my father was minimal from the start, and what little there had been had ebbed. My father had accepted her lack of passion, as he had accepted the twin beds. Did her hauteur sadden and disappoint him? I imagined so. Did he attribute her reserve to the love she still felt for her first husband? Probably so. My mother had been respectful in her behavior toward my father, at least until the end, careful to protect him from reminders of her former marriage. But a gulf existed between them that they did not bridge. She was not affectionate. They had held hands once in my presence—at least there was a brief clasp. I remembered that my father was steadying her after a stumble.

Now in the dusk he sat in the green chair, curtly laying out a long history of accommodations to my mother's wishes. She had insisted he move into the house in Catasauqua where she and Tommy had lived. I had not known my parents ever lived there.

"Of course, there were reasons," he said. "She wanted to minimize the disruption for the girls. And there was some economic necessity." A bed is not just the site of passion, I mused; it is where couples console one another, where they soothe headaches and souls, where they embrace against the world. It is where they share small successes and greater triumphs, quietly reliving the good of their shared life. This my parents had not had. They had not taken their disappointments and sorrows to bed and expiated them, taken their joys and celebrated them. Alone they had lain in their single beds, for better or for worse.

She insisted that her first husband's relatives be included in holiday celebrations, my father was saying, though they never blessed the remarriage. Christmases were a curse. "Was she unhappy? I thought she was happy. What about all the trips we took? Your mother loved to travel." He was musing disconnectedly. "Was our marriage a sham?" he asked, as if I were an impersonal bystander, not their daughter, as if their marital woes had played no role in my life.

"She said she hated me." The hatred she felt seemed to have existed for years, reaching far back into the past. If words can touch skin, then my father's words abraded my face.

"Daddy, it was the Alzheimer's talking," I answered. But I wasn't sure. I only felt sure that we would have to forgive her, and I did not know if we could. I longed for her mercy, and my father's mercy too. But there was no mercy. Not for me, nor my father, not for anyone who lies in the bed of an unjoined heart.

The Structure of Trouble

Some think of trouble

> as difficulty, as something to be overcome. **Examples:** I'm having some trouble untying this knot. I'm experiencing some trouble getting into my kayak. I'm having some trouble getting my horse to move forward.

> > The assumption is that a remedy is available: the knot can be untied, you can be assisted into the kayak, the horse can be moved forward from its stopped position.

> as the negative consequence of unwise or forbidden behavior. **Examples:** Pregnancy as the consequence of unprotected sex; traffic ticket as the consequence of speeding.

> > **Personal example:** In eighth grade, my science teacher, Mr. Samuels, warned me to stop pumping my leg. I had trouble (as in difficulty) keeping still in my seat for the whole period and I jiggled my leg *aggressively*, according to Mr. Samuels, scissor kicking, he called it. He warned me that if I didn't stop, there would be negative consequences. I didn't stop. I couldn't stop. Mr. Samuels took down the wood paddle hanging on the wall near the blackboard and paddled me in front of the class.

> as when someone or something behaves in such a consistently *troubling* manner that she becomes synonymous with the word *trouble*. **Examples:** My friend Martha has a puppy who so regularly misbehaves that instead of calling the puppy by her name, Louise, Martha says, "Here comes Trouble." Or a kitten named Trouble because he was repeatedly found caught in the toilet bowl.

as a specific event of a certain duration that causes distress, that disturbs the heretofore tranquil waters of our life. **Examples:** bad news (that can be gotten over), a fight (that will be resolved), a storm (that will pass through).

Question: But what if trouble is something larger than a fight or a storm or a piece of bad news? What if it's a depth we plumb? What if it isn't an event but something that lives in the body and, like the blues, it comes upon us, it comes over us and we don't know when or if it will pass?

Women may get the blues;
Men are more likely to get a bullet
Through the temple.[1]

How Trouble Feels

It feels like a headache. Even though I don't get headaches, that's what I say when it's too hard to describe what I feel like when trouble comes, when I'm heartsick and want to lie down, when I can't stand up to the day before me. A headache is an acceptable reason to lie down in the middle of the day, or so it seems in my experience. Who says, *I can't stand up anymore* to her boss, her teacher, her paramour? No one who wants to keep her job. Complicated excuses or explanations that require interpretation don't cut it in the workaday world.

What You Can't Say

You can't say: *It's a blue afternoon suddenly and I've got to lie down.*

---

[1] Barbara Ehrenreich, "Did Feminism Make Women Miserable?" *Salon.com*, October 15, 2009.

You can't say: *For some reason I can't pinpoint, I'm remembering something that happened to one of my best friends in ninth grade who rode horses with me. How one night that year, horses at the stable were left out in the pasture when they shouldn't have been, despite tornado warnings. How in the storm the horses broke out of the fenced pasture and ran as a group onto the highway where because of the storm and the dark drivers couldn't see. Some of them were hit and killed and my friend's horse was among them.*

Question: I don't know why I am sometimes visited by this memory. Does the memory make me low or does my state of lowness trigger the memory? Which comes first? I never picture their deaths—just the running and the blood draining from their brains, and then my friend getting smaller and smaller, shrinking into a wizened old woman, shrinking into someone I could hardly recognize from the girl I once knew.

Warning: It will not go well for you if you say anything like this. People will think you are unbalanced and given to visitations. The untroubled mask must always be fitted closely to your face while in public.

What You Can Say

A literal medical condition is required. That's what people understand and accept. In my experience, females are incapacitated by migraines on a regular basis. All manner of female has employed the headache to get out of whatever she was supposed to be doing, to craft an exit.

Most Frequent Time of Visitation

No doubt this a subjective calculation; some might say from dusk to dawn, the hours of darkness, what some people call the sinking time. But not me. I say late afternoon. At least that's when it begins to make its first appearance.

Right now as the dinner hour approaches, women are lying down all over the world. I can hear the collective sigh of mattresses as they lie down with their loneliness, with whatever fells them.

Personal history: I've only known one man to claim a headache before dinner and that was my husband, Richard, who said his head hurt after he slipped on the black ice of our driveway and hit his head so hard he knocked himself out. That's what it took for him to say he had a headache and needed to lie down. Men do other things when trouble comes upon them. But those things are not what I think about when I think about trouble. I don't get headaches; I don't know why. I'm not complaining, mind you, I just find it odd to have the quintessential female affliction pass me by.

How It Feels to Me

Imagine a line of dancers, a chorus line, all moving to the same relentless beat with no appearance of difficulty and suddenly one of the dancers falls out of step, she's a beat off, a beat slow, and then two beats, and soon she staggers out of the line altogether and must grab hold of the velvet curtain backstage to keep from collapsing. What came over her, you ask. Who can say exactly, but she needs to go lie down immediately.

That's how it is for me. One moment I'm fine, moving in the rhythm, in the line, in the chorus, until I'm not. I call what happens a falling, a staggering,
but rather than falter, my heart flutters, a kind of stuttering rhythm, like a blue moth flapping from side to side inside my chest, caught in an existential corner.

Origins

The trouble with troubled relationships is they are troubled. And when the relationship is with one's parents, and especially one's mother, and has been troubled since birth, or so it feels, then one's whole life is framed by this trouble.

> **Personal backstory:** My parents never spoke of the circumstances surrounding my birth. No baby pictures were taken. No baby book, where the milestones are recorded, exists. One winter evening after dinner while we were washing the dishes, I asked my mother what she remembered about my birth. "Well," she said, taken aback by the sudden question, "you were a small baby, only five pounds and you had to stay in the hospital for two weeks before you could come home."
>
> "Was there anything wrong with me?"
>
> "Nothing lasting," she said as she wiped the counter for the second time. I couldn't understand why she didn't want to tell me about my birth, why she seemed to be keeping something from me.
>
> "Do you remember anything else?" I asked.
>
> She said, "You weren't born as planned," and looked at me hard, as if an old anger had been stirred out of the corner. "You were two weeks past your due date and in the middle of the night my water broke."
>
> I didn't have the foggiest idea what she meant by waters breaking. Was she being metaphorical about not being able to hold me inside

her any longer? She seemed angry, angry at me. The words *plan, water breaking* were parts of a puzzle called my birth that I had to assemble.

"Anything else?"

That was it. She was done telling me the story of my birth. She hung her apron on the handle of the oven door and joined my father in the den to watch the nightly news.

My mother's defensiveness on the subject of my birth led me to believe that the day, the event, my first entrance onto the stage and into my mother's life, was complicated by emotions I didn't understand and might never understand. I came to think that from my mother's point of view my birth was a mistake and that was why all the memorializing forms were blank.

Causes (1): I sometimes think of my life as one long attempt, and failure, to right the wrong-footed relationship I've had with my mother. One strategy after another, with the same result: failure. Hoping that some miracle of understanding would occur, that the origin of the trouble between us would be exposed, worked through, and put behind us— bridges would span across broken waters, hands would meet.

> **Aside:** There is an annoying resiliency in this hopeful fantasy. Despite all evidence to the contrary, hope springs eternal that we can fix things that have gone wrong even when we don't understand why they went wrong in the first place. I can't say how many times and with what vehemence I've tried to bury this hope, cremate it and scatter its ashes, set it on a leaking vessel and shove it out to sea, kick it into the deepest hole one can dig on this earth, throw it down a bottomless well. To no avail. Turn around,

and there it is, hope, fresh and potent as new-mown hay, a pasture full of it.

Causes (2): Then there's the matter of my mother's trouble, how it affected me, how I struggled to understand it.

Repeated Scene

In the late afternoon my mother used to retire to the bedroom and lie down on her twin bed, whose cool mint spread was permanently unwrinkled. (My parents did not sleep in the same bed; that in itself is a disturbing fact and may have contributed to my mother's malaise.)

> **Interruption:** I have found little to be optimistic about in the facts that my parents slept in separate beds during their whole marriage and that my mother was obsessive about keeping her bedspread unwrinkled.

Her retirement often followed on the heels of my return home from school. She'd follow me into the kitchen, where I was stealing an after-school snack, open the refrigerator door, and bend over to peer inside as if the shelves were the dimly lit walls of a cave and she had no idea what lived there. She seemed a bit frightened. She'd turn to me, with hands on her thin jutting hips, and ask in a quivering voice, "What do you think I should make for dinner?" I would suggest a few items she regularly made—meatloaf, mustard chicken, seven-layer casserole, and all of them angered her for reasons I have struggled to understand. In a huff, she'd throw open the cabinets above the stove and look behind the boxes of crackers and cereal as if she'd discover a murder weapon. (The anger didn't last; maybe it would have been better if it had. Anger often keeps one from collapse. But as I said, her anger would subside, and collapse would come.) Finding nothing, she'd put the boxes back into their places and say, "Just thinking about dinner gives me a headache.

I'm going to lie down for a few minutes." Down the beige hall to her bedroom she's pad, trouble incarnate, and then she'd close her door.

It was never a few minutes.

The other character in the drama of the repeated scene was my father.

> He would arrive home from work expecting dinner to be in preparation, if not ready, and instead he would find my mother lying down.

>> **Aside:** When I hear people say that feminism makes women unhappy and it would be better to return to the good old days when men and women knew their places, I want to beat my head against the wall. They didn't live in my house where my father knew his place (he had the job, made the money, and expected to have dinner served to him by my mother or some female substitute at the end of the day) and my mother knew hers (she was supposed to oversee meals, specifically dinner). It had been decided by my parents under the watchful eye of the god of matrimony that dinner had to take place at the same time each day, 6:00 o'clock sharp, or else. This was the meal grid.

> My father never went to my mother to see what the trouble was. Instead he sat in the living room supposedly reading the paper, but secretly watching the sun set over the icy fields and river curving like a question mark below our house.

>> **Question:** What was he thinking? He was probably wondering how long this latest spell of my mother's would last. Would she open the bedroom door and emerge ready to

make dinner, or would she stay wrapped in her mint green spread until morning?

On these occasions my father did not endeavor to feed himself or me, rustling up cheese and crackers, at the very least. No. He slumped in his lounge chair, looking out into the dark that had fallen, until he concluded my mother would not be putting in an appearance.

Third Character in Repeated Scene (Like Mother, Like Daughter, the Chain of Substitution)

Eventually he called me into the living room, and without any preamble, asked: *Will dinner be ready any time soon?*

On these evenings I made a box of something, usually macaroni and cheese, brought my father his bowl, and took my own portion into my room where I disappeared for the rest of the night. I padded heavily down the same beige hallway as my mother, trouble incarnate, following her foot impressions in the plush pile.

Conclusion of Repeated Scene

I never heard my father enter the bedroom they shared.

> **Lingering question:** Why did my mother not think she had the wherewithal to refuse dinner, to alter the marital script so as to alleviate her anxiety? Suppose a documentary were made and the filmmaker pulled my mother aside and asked her, "What do you really think about dinner?" My mother, if she were truthful, would look into the camera and say, "I hate it!" And once she uttered those three little words, she'd say

more. There might be no end to what she'd say about women and dinner and marriage and other things that troubled her. My mother never said any of these things and I don't know why.

Mystery and Manners

The next morning my mother gave some explanation for her disappearance. *She had a headache* was one of her usual ones. Sometimes she said, "I'm so tired," in a threadbare voice that baffled me. I couldn't understand what tired her, what made it so hard to get through the late afternoon and dinner. It seemed to me at that early age that my mother had nothing to do all day, and I envied her freedom. I couldn't fathom why my father's expectation that my mother make dinner caused her to fall apart.

As a child I did not understand the mysteries of marital relations and adult disappointment.

Even now I don't know why my mother never found something to devote herself to, something that was hers. The gap between my mother's promise and the outcome, between the talented and spirited mother I knew and the mother who decided to lie down is a mystery I haven't solved.

But the explanation for her disappearance that unnerved me the most was when she said, "I don't feel like myself," and then looked into her coffee cup as if it might be poisoned.

Question: What did that mean? Whom did she feel like? Was she referring to marriage as a body-snatching experience?

Fear

I fear my heartsickness is a variation of my mother's "I don't feel like myself." When I lie down in the late afternoon, I worry that what ails me, what's come over me, is my mother. I fear that I am my mother, that I, too, am susceptible to the gap between promise and outcome, between how things should be and how things are. There's a pause, of some hours, when the machinery of my life breaks down. I don't know what to call it, this low, this trouble. My body slows down, but not my brain. My brain goes *Drive on* while I'm lying on my side, holding myself like a clenched fist, like a bud that will not open. I turn toward the sliding glass doors looking out into the backyard. Nothing moves but my eyes. They blink and blink again.

I don't know why I absorb other people's trouble, the sorrow that leaks out of car windows and suitcases at the passenger drop-off. But I do. Maybe it's because I grew up trying to understand my mother. It started young, this absorbing of trouble, taking it in, making it mine. It started with my mother.

Fall

I feel the need to lie down most in the autumn of the year. It's then that my heart feels like a sore. I feel a shifting in my chest, the way a rose, once soft and unfolding, begins to harden into a fist with the first frost. And the visitations begin.

> Often my father stands on my front stoop in a beige and stained raincoat, the collar turned up, his glasses fogged, with an

attaché case extended from his arm. I open the door and he grabs my arm and moves us through the vestibule with a sense of urgency I can't understand. He sets the attaché case on the kitchen counter and removes a slip of paper, which he waves before my face. Written there is his age and the number of times I've visited in the last ten years. One sum is large and one sum is embarrassingly small. "How much time do you think I have left?" he says.

I leave my father in the kitchen but he follows me into the bedroom. He does not remove his raincoat, his shoes drip steadily into the carpet.

I'd like to drift off to sleep before anyone else shows up, but my mother sprawls on the bed beside me. "You called," she says. "No, I didn't call you." Just like old times, we argue while my father stands dripping and waving the slip of paper. My heart feels it can't take much more before it bursts inside my chest. When will my father trudge back to his retirement home? When will my mother return to her grave? When will the ice thaw on the river?

> **Question**: Could it be that when my mother said she didn't feel like herself, she actually felt most like herself? That the opposite of what she said was true? On those late afternoons was the mask showing that everything was okay breaking down?

Everything wasn't okay and for a few hours, or maybe longer, she couldn't open her eyes.

It's just the opposite for me. I lie down like my mother and I want to close my eyes like my mother, but I can't. They just stay open.

The Stronger One

It used to be that her father was the most important fact about a girl like me. All to follow in her life would grow from that root cause—the world according to fathers. Such would not be the case with my life, I resolved, and so I made you small in the stories I told of it. In them you are a secondary character, minor to others' major status.

I didn't *decide* to relegate you to a supporting role, little better than a butler who holds the door for a gaudy entrance by the star. I didn't sit at my desk on the third floor looking out over the treetops and say, "Goodbye, Daddy." Yet it happened. You pop up in character roles, but the story is never about you, never an engagement with you. You aren't entirely absent; I didn't delete you. But our relationship is a stripped thing, glanced at on the way to the main event. I had to do it that way, really. If I hadn't pushed you into a corner, you would have gobbled up the scenery like a tacky actor. Had I allowed you a prominent role, my attention would have been derailed from the essential topic, my titanic struggles with Mother. She and my half sisters, the woman-center of the household, were my flood subject, the waters breaking and the bloody show, blending in a single tide.

Around Which We Pivoted

It was tempting to imagine a dramatic and symbolically rich death for you, but alas, you were not a soldier or a diplomat serving the country on long absences from home. No train you rode derailed and plunged off a bridge. Truth requires I admit that you were a daily, predictable presence in our lives. And yet because of the arrangement of your marriage and family life, you remained outside the core, never quite welcomed in. You may have paid for the house, but it wasn't yours.

We daughters attended to our mother intensely, as the floodlit center around which we pivoted. We suffered you—that's the script I followed, taking my cue from those older and wiser than I. Of course, I wasn't entirely welcomed into the mother-sisters unit either. You and I were Aldriches, and they were not.

Our shared blood and outside orbit might have been a consoling bond between us, but it was not. I reminded you of your own status in Mother's affections. Neither you nor I was what she wanted, a deficiency neither of us cared to admit we shared. You saw, or could have seen, in her ill-disguised disdain for me her distaste for you. And I didn't want to see my fate in yours—as someone Mother suffered. There were many strategies through which we could keep the truth of our fate at bay.

Visitor at the Gates

Each of the daughters had her own bedroom, and privacy was more valuable than communal closeness. We had places we could retreat to, where we became acquainted with ourselves; only you and Mother shared a room, though you did not share a bed.

Your money was hers, so you said, though she had to ask permission to spend it and had to demonstrate gratitude in return. Prosperity shaped our lives. Mother made the daily decisions about the house and children, and it isn't surprising that in a household of girls she should be the center of our world, or that you should be peripheral, a visitor knocking at the gates.

Mother admitted you entrance and endured your presence because it was what women did to support themselves. She did not have a job in the conventional sense, outside the home. You were her job, and she had to manage you, as if a difficult client. Did she bear you affection or love? Maybe; I'm not sure. It was impossible to disentangle her dependence upon you from her natural feelings. She was grateful, I can say that.

I struggled with my feelings as well, for it was through your financial generosity that many things I valued came to me. Because of you I have been well educated. But I've felt more gratitude than love for you, since you never let me forget I was in your debt.

D.K.A.

At summer camp in the Poconos I received a few communications from you—business cards filled out by your secretary and signed with your initials, *D.K.A.* Shortened by removal of the middle initial, this became my name for you, *D.A.* Formal, unloving, it denoted a larval version of the relationship of father to child often called *Daddy*.

Ring!

We had two telephones in the house. The first, a beige wall phone, hung near the swinging door between the kitchen and the dining room. The second phone resided in the upstairs hallway on a white table next to a little matching chair with a seat cover embroidered with birds in flight. Four bedrooms and a bathroom opened out onto the hall.

You normally spoke on the phone in the kitchen. Your conversations were of the shortest duration and usually related to business. But on the Fourth of July, when I was six years old, the phone rang in the middle of the night, or so it seemed, for I had long been asleep in my bed. The ringing shattered the silence of the house, and you stumbled out of bed and flung open the bedroom door with a force I feared would wrench it from its hinges. Then your voice was low and troubling, the call longer than your usual curt transactions. Finally you said, "Thank you for calling," and you hung up. I got out of bed and came into the hall, where you were slumped in the embroidered chair, hand still resting on the phone's mouthpiece. Something terrible had happened, and you were shaken. We were joined by Mother, who turned on the hall light, and my sisters appeared. We stood in our nightclothes, hair disheveled, and looked at you, ungirded by your robe or slippers. It was the first time we had formed an arc around you in the middle of the night.

Your only uncle had died, and now you would shoulder the burden of my grandmother alone. (In your third year of college, your father died. You dropped out, found work, and began to support your mother. Your uncle had helped.) I saw how death shook you. It was my first death, and from then on, for me, that news came in the night and carried you with it. Its razor ring shears sleep, severing lives into before and after. I remember you—exasperated, impatient, wanting to get on with it, whatever it was.

Like a Son to Me

Weekdays, you rose early, left the house to have breakfast with your friends and associates, and returned home at dinnertime. As a life insurance salesman you often made house calls at night. I have little memory of your presence in the evening when I was young. As you became more successful and the business changed, house calls became a thing of the past, and you were at home, reading or watching television with Mother. On weekends you played golf with friends, attended church, and visited your mother. You led a remarkably independent life—plotting your schedule of activities as you chose, touching down for dinner and other duties you performed with your wife. You weren't woven into the fabric of our days. You didn't enter my bedroom to speak with me. I didn't seek you out for advice or ask a question about math. You were not my counselor.

Mother never voiced a longing to see more of you or complained that you weren't around. No, just the opposite: she was glad you departed early in the morning and left her to her own devices. And so was I. When you returned, we felt oppressed; heaviness hung at the center of the house, clogging the main arteries to Mother.

You made but brief appearances in my stories of growing up. You stood on the clubhouse veranda in a blue seersucker suit after the conclusion of your workday, watching with chagrin my commotion in the pool below, splashing in a stroke of my own design. You were there to pick me up on your way home from work, and you got a glimpse of my ineptitude. I hurt your sense of what a swimmer should be, for it was you who harbored the desire that I be a competitor and follow in your footsteps. You pushed me into sports as fathers direct their sons, projecting their own wishes onto the boy and living vicariously through him.

It was you who, returning one Sunday night after a weekend trip, learned that my leg was swollen from a bicycle accident on Friday. I had ridden recklessly down a hill and run into a tree. You took me to the hospital for x-rays. I had broken my leg, and Mother declined to notice. Daughters were not supposed to ride a bike recklessly or fall from trees or require medical attention. Mother cared nothing about my swimming or any other athletic endeavor. She cared about how I looked; that was what females should properly be concerned with.

You weren't interested in who I was or what I felt, whether I felt loved or whether I suffered, but it was you who was interested in my advancement. You cared where I placed in the swim meet and the horse show. You were interested in what grades I earned, my class rank, what programs or schools admitted me. You didn't care nearly as much about my sisters' progress. You assumed they would find husbands at college, marry, and become stay-at-home mothers in the pattern set out by Mother. And they did. For my sisters college was a finishing school, a place to meet good mates and train for the place in the social world that awaited them. These attitudes didn't hold with me. Times were changing and assumptions about a girl's development were breaking down. You treated me like a son you were grooming to assume responsibility for his own life.

Drop Shot

In teaching me tennis you used the drop shot strategically. Once I had progressed beyond the airy returns of a beginner, I liked to hit hard, flat strokes, loath to leave the baseline, where I felt good on my feet, secure. Out of nowhere you'd hit a dink that just crossed the net and plummeted to earth like a dead bird. If I hurled myself at the net, I still could not get my racket on the ball with its fading bounce. A tennis naïf, uncertain of my footing except in the safe zone far from the net, I never saw it coming. *The court is more than the baseline,* you would say. *Learn about the space at the front of the court.* You would not coddle, hit soft balls to my feet, you said.

I found it mean-spirited. You were a skilled man playing against an unskilled girl. Did you need cheap shots to win? And was winning so very important? You and your drop shot were trickery.

Eventually I learned about touch and soft hands and how to let go just when you want to squeeze hard. You taught me the harsh lesson, pulling me to the net like a puppet and then lobbing a volley over my head. But I became cunning in my own way.

The Dole

I shared Mother's dependency, but my response was contrary. I vowed to depend on no one for my financial well-being. The cost was too high—a debt one could never repay, a ledger one could never clear. Or so it seemed if I judged according to the example of our family. Mother's leisure held no appeal. Not for a minute did I aspire to be taken care of. I wanted a job and money of my own. You were my model, not Mother, though that fact was hidden from me for a long time.

I worked hard not to see how much I was like you. I didn't want to be reminded that I was the product of a second marriage and didn't share the same father, the same genetic makeup with my sisters. I wanted to belong with them, not you, and yet it was you I took after.

Erasure

You and Mother didn't like to look closely at things; a passing glance was the family way. Erasure and denial were your modus operandi. You constructed your own realities, your own stories of family events and dynamics to suit your own needs, and to my eye they were fictions. Unpleasant fights, harsh scarring words—these were blotted from the family ledger, and a new account would be written over the one I fervently believed. That rewritten version would then take its place as the family edition, and what actually happened was banished. But I didn't accept these omissions. Someone had to counter all that fiction-making with another story.

An example, a story to revisit, one written and crossed out, deleted and restored: When I was in college I accompanied you on a spring vacation at a tennis colony on the Florida coast. In my version of the story, I would include your history of losing your temper when things did not go your way. You broke tennis rackets and golf clubs—breaking something was a routine response to frustration.

We were playing singles at the busy complex, and all the courts were full. You weren't satisfied with your level of play. You weren't happy that I was beating you. You swore at me and smashed your racket on the court. I was embarrassed by the spectacle you were making in this public place. Players on nearby courts were watching us. I told you that I was done and going back to our cottage.

"You can't do that," you said. "You can't walk off the courts until I say you can." (In your version of the story, you would explain

what I did that was so infuriating. But you never told it, and I don't
know what I did.)

With you I had studied serve and volley in the game of
anger, so I left the court and hurried down the lane to our cottage.
You huffed and puffed behind me, angrier and angrier. By the time
we reached our cottage, where Mother was reading on the porch,
you had lost control. I ran inside and you followed and you grabbed
my neck with your hands. Mother had to pry your hands loose from
my neck. You broke your watch in the scuffle. A lamp was knocked
over and a shower curtain pulled from its rod.

The fight occurred midweek in our vacation. We did not
pack our bags and go home. We stuck it out. That night we went
to a French restaurant that had been recommended to you. I was
too heartsick to eat and tried to refuse, but my refusals were
ineffectual.

Meanwhile, you ate well, as if nothing of import had
happened earlier—as if your hands now holding a fork were not the
same hands that had squeezed my neck. We were parents and
daughter, a happy threesome, on a Florida vacation, having dinner
at an elegant restaurant. For all the feeling you showed about me,
I might have been a cardboard daughter propped up at the table
with the fancy linen tablecloth.

In subsequent years, whenever the trip was recalled, you
would marvel over the delicious meal, saying, "Marcia, do you
remember that quaint French restaurant we ate at?" You had
erased the events of the afternoon, erased the profound unhappiness
of our family life, erased your problems with anger.

No, that is not what I remember. I thought I was losing my
mind, and that no one would ever confirm or believe what actually
happened inside my family.

Now I ponder your rage. Why all that anger directed
toward me, unleashed upon me? When I was young, I simply didn't
understand it. I was baffled by your ill treatment of me, your only
offspring. I did not understand that my resemblance to you, my role
as bearer of dreams and ally in sufferance, made me the target of
your wrath, frustration, even self-loathing. It was as if you were
smashing your self-image that you found in me.

What's in a Name? (I)

Given your pride in our family name—you owned a three-volume history of the Aldriches—you might have been pleased that I chose to keep my maiden name when I married in my mid-twenties. It was mine, given to me at birth, the name I had scrawled at the top of my papers and poems for years, the name I had answered to when called all my life. My husband's last name was Finnish (Isomaki) and overvoweled and didn't speak to me. I disliked the look and sound of it when combined with Marcia. I had come too far, gone far too long with the sound of *Aldrich* to give the name up just because I was getting married. It was a mistake I had made before.

I was your only birth child, the only child to carry your name, and I reasoned that you would be happy with my decision to continue the name, keep the family name alive. But you weren't. The rule of power and custom far exceeded your pride in your own name and your respect for my proclaimed wishes. You refused to acknowledge that I had not taken my husband's name. From the day of our wedding, all correspondence, gifts, checks for children's birthdays and Christmas gifts were addressed to a woman who did not exist. It was an opportunity for you to claim me as yours in a different way.

I sent back correspondence addressed to that woman, with the name crossed out and *Aldrich* written over it. On one occasion I penned words in bold, saying, *No such person lives here.* I was shrill, frantic perhaps, to get you to call me by my name, the name you had given me. I might have let the matter go, turned it into a light, humorous anecdote about the unfinished progress of woman's liberation, but your refusal to acknowledge my wishes irked me and was a wedge between us. Given the opportunity to support your adult daughter's strongly argued wishes, you chose to refuse me.

Timed to the Minute

For the bulk of our lives we spoke infrequently on the phone, and on those occasions the exchange was brief.

As a grown woman, if I called and you happened to answer, you'd say, "Your mother will fill me in" or "I assume you are all right."

I'd say, "Yes, I'm fine."

Then you'd grunt, "Good." And there would be an implied goodbye. Gruff and businesslike, that was your manner. It was Mother to whom I spoke.

In the years of her decline, during Mother's dementia, she was incapable of talking on the phone, and you were forced to answer my calls. You began to move to the center of the frame. Sometimes you even called me when despair and frustration overtook you. These calls came in the afternoon when Mother was napping and you thought it safe to have a conversation about her. You seldom left her alone. You were trapped together in the condo. You preferred to suffer the claustrophobia of confinement rather than admit that Mother was suffering from dementia. But there were days when she said things that hurt you. On these days you called. You wanted me to listen to you—this is what you always wanted from me—to listen. If I suggested a remedy or intervention, you became irritated and closed out the call. *Click.* You were gone.

What's in a Name? (II)

In Mother's obituary, written by you, I was listed as *Mrs. Marcia Respectable Woman Who Bears Her Husband's Last Name*, although you misspelled his last name, confused by all those vowels. How ironic, I bitterly seethed, you can't even spell the name you are so intent upon giving me.

I began my campaign with you anew. I thought that without Mother's influence reinforcing the conventional approach, you could be brought around to my family name—your name. Periodically, when I received a card addressed to Marcia Aldrich, I believed I had succeeded and that Mother had been the real obstacle all along. But then, a card would come addressed to Marcia Respectable Woman Who Bears Her Husband's Last Name, and I wondered what had caused the relapse, whether the effort to honor my wishes, even in something so easy and fundamental, was too much for you to sustain.

Punctuality

After her death, you took to phoning me regularly. After her death, you were ready to turn to me, and you called every Saturday morning at 8:30. I resented these calls. You never inquired when a good time to call was, when might suit my schedule. You had long been retired and it never occurred to you that 8:30 a.m. on Saturday, the beginning of my weekend, was not an opportune time to call, that I might wish to sleep later or lounge about doing whatever I pleased, drinking my coffee, drifting free on the eddies of time. But it had never occurred to you to consider me in the equation at all. You kept busy in old age and calling me was part of your Saturday schedule. Eight-thirty suited you. It filled in the dead space between breakfast and your Saturday errands.

I felt tempted not to answer, but you picked your time well. At 8:30 in the morning it was hard not to answer your calls. I could not find excuses. Where would I be at that hour other than at home? If I didn't answer, you would call again and again, and the rings would fill the house with their insistent need. Your relentlessness always wore me down. At last I'd answer, and you'd angrily demand to know why I hadn't answered earlier, and I'd make up an excuse, pathetic as that of a six-year-old. It was easier just to answer the call at 8:30.

I was caught between my anger toward you and my sense of duty, and I never was able to manage a compromise between the two or happy solution. Which was worse—to feel guilty about refusing you, my father, or to feel trampled by you?

The High Pitch of the Female Voice

You called, but you had no interest in me. If I spoke of my life, you couldn't hear the words. Hard of hearing for much of your life, you had perfected a technique of tuning out the females around you. In old age you claimed the high pitch of the female voice was difficult to pick up. You didn't wear hearing aids while talking on the phone with me. I'm not sure why. I suspected that because you had no real interest in hearing what I said, you didn't attempt to get your hearing aids to work on the phone. Whether you couldn't hear or weren't inclined to listen, the result was the same: your phone calls were delivered monologues, usually accounts of your health. You never tired of updating me on how you felt, the latest test results, your doctor's appointments. After all, what you wanted to hear was the sound of your own voice.

By the end of a call, I wanted to smash the phone against the wall.

What's in a Name? (III)

When you died, and we began to manage the considerable paperwork of your estate, I discovered that "herein" and "hereafter" I was referred to as Marcia Respectable Woman Who Bears Her Husband's Last Name and that you never did get the spelling of his name right. The ironies piled up. First, you insisted on imposing a name upon me that belonged to my husband, who himself had never penetrated your consciousness in all the years of our marriage. You knew next to nothing about him, spoke the scantest words to him when by chance he answered the phone, and still you imposed his name upon my own. Yet you got the spelling wrong—wrong on all the documentation you carefully assembled before your death.

It's only fitting that troubles arose over your estate because you insisted on wrongly naming me. I had no legal status as Marcia Respectable Woman Who Bears Her Husband's Last Name, no driver's license, no checking account. I could get no forms notarized or processed in that persona. Every form had to be altered with the added words "also known as Marcia Aldrich."

Ring! Ring!

After a week's vacation in Florida with my sister and her husband, the three of you drove the last leg back to their home in Lancaster, Pennsylvania. You didn't tarry to share a few recollections of the week's events but stepped into your car and drove the seventy miles to Allentown, not an arduous drive normally, but perhaps taxing as the capstone to a full day of travel. You stopped at the grocery store to purchase a few essentials—not much, for you never bought more than you could carry in one bag. You pulled into the long sweeping drive of Luther Crest, the retirement community where you lived after Mother died, and parked in your spot near the entrance. With your groceries and luggage in tow, you took the elevator to the third floor, turned right toward the long corridor to your apartment. You walked with difficulty, a shuffling step, past one closed door after another, each with a number and name in small print in a brass frame above the doorbell. Outside each door was a ledge with displays, vases of plastic flowers, snow globes covered in dust, animal figurines with big eyes. You always liked dogs, were affectionate with our English cocker, Irene. I wonder if you glanced at the dogs with momentous eyes and realized they were trying to speak to you, a story you ought to hear.

Inside your apartment, you called my sister, said you had arrived home and were okay. You exchanged a few pleasantries with her about the trip. You unpacked your light travel kit, put your wallet and watch in the top dresser drawer, where I found them later, read your mail, made a snack, called Pat, the woman you took up with after Mother died, whom we hadn't met because you thought she might affront our memory (no, we were glad for you, Daddy!), and made plans to see her the next day.

Shortly after nine you had a heart attack. The nitroglycerin spray you carried did nothing to help you breathe. The attack continued, for it was your time. You called the first responder, who quickly called the paramedics. But you were punctual in death as in life.

Several hours later, our phone rang. My husband answered and handed over the phone, saying, "Your sister." I knew what important news she had to tell at this special time. The heat had shut off for the night, and it was cold in the bedroom. Outside the snow fell lightly.

When the call was over, I stepped out to our small deck in the back. I remembered how you had hastened away from the gravesite where we buried Mother's ashes, trying to get to your car as fast as you could. The day before you had bought a cheap suit on sale and it wasn't the proper size because you wouldn't try it on. Who buys a suit without trying it on? It was too small and it was too late to get another—you had to wear it. The buttons were popping and the seams unraveling as the brief burial service took place. You were trying to get to your car before the suit fell apart. You were holding the lapels as you walked across the gravel.

The Stronger One

After Mother died, I wondered if you felt the lack of father-to-child communication, and if so, whether it disturbed your peace of mind. Did you lie awake at night worrying that you had failed me, and wonder if you could ever make it right?

From the evidence, I don't think so. You had trouble sleeping but worry over me was not the cause. You were aware we had a poor relationship, but you didn't dwell on it. There may have been moments of recrimination and regret. With Pat you might have gone over certain decisions you'd make differently. Or you may not have mentioned me, except to relate the bare facts of my existence. She may have inquired why you saw me so infrequently, or she may have kept her thoughts to herself. If asked, you'd probably cite work or financial limitations as the reasons I didn't visit. You would not look at the heart of my absence from your life and reveal its darkness to her.

When I met her at your memorial service, I expected someone in the mold of Mother, haughty and withholding, someone you couldn't really have. But she wasn't anything like Mother. She was petite, deeply tanned, and wore copious amounts of blue eye shadow. Her step was quick, her manner easy, and when we met at the punch bowl, we extended a hand to each other at the same time. Seeing something open in her face, I thought she might reveal your feelings for me—that is what I wanted. But she had nothing to tell me.

I don't think I was an important personage in your life. You weren't as troubled by the failure of our bond as I would have liked you to be; you weren't as troubled as I was. It was I who felt bereft of love, I who lacked something important. Are children more haunted by the lack of parental love than parents who are not loved by their children? Children depend upon their parents for everything—neglect can create a temperament that can't easily be changed. I was low on your list of priorities, a kind of accessory to your real life. Mother was the person who mattered to you. You spent your life trying to give her what she wanted, and you failed. It was my mother's side that you took in fights with me. After a fight in which my mother broke down in tears, blamed me for all the trouble, and then vanished into the bedroom, you'd come to me, even when I was a child, and tell me that she was fragile, that I was the stronger one. *The stronger one.* How I longed for you to fight for me, to shore me up. You allowed her to hurt me, no doubt the way she hurt you.

Perhaps I've downsized you in retaliation.

Ring! Ring! Ring!

Searching for a number, I scroll down the contact list past "Father." The entry was programmed by my husband on an earlier phone of mine and has moved with the rest of memory as it has been transferred from device to device.

Why do I keep you in this trivial cache of recollection? You are no longer available to receive calls, and you cannot disturb a sunny Saturday morning. Your service has been disconnected for eternity.

I have my mother's plates and amethyst ring, my grandmother's drop-leaf side table. These are items I use or wear, touch or dust, to bring the plangent memories back to me. I haven't things of yours; with you I have only a name. You who were never one to linger, yet I cannot delete you. *D.K.A. a.k.a. Daddy.*

She and I (A Field of Force)

Breathless

I should have known what I was up against, what the future held, right then. I should have known that whatever step I took with her, in whatever mood, with whatever intention, whether reward or punishment, whether acceptance or rejection or simple love, would prove futile. She would be who she was, and there would be no changing her. There would only be the spectacle of my thwarting her.

All was revealed in that moment many years ago, had I been able to understand its meaning.

She was playing with a boy named Sam, whose house she had never visited before. I had arrived to pick her up, Sam's mother, with whom my husband had a slight professional acquaintance, walked me around to the back. There in the sandbox were the children, absorbed in play, constructing their dreams with plastic shovels and buckets and toy dump trucks. The other mother and I paused in the grass a few feet away, exchanging stiff pleasantries until the time should seem right to disentangle Clare and get her round to the front of the house.

After five minutes or so, the moment came. "Honey, it's time to go," I began.

She was pouring water out of a bright blue bucket into a moat surrounding a sandy castle. Her motions implied only that she was having a good time. There was no indication that circumstances permitted human communications of any sort. I was about to repeat my sentence when, working at the moat exactly as before, she uttered the word "no." It was almost disembodied. There was no shading to it, nothing of the delicate, high vaults in the cathedral of social bonds. It could not have been more blunt.

Sam, sensing a dangerous fray in the making, pulled himself smaller. He kept pushing his little truck across the sand, but the motion had lost all spontaneity. He lifted his eyes to watch my next move.

"It is time to go," I said more firmly.

More firmly still, and now with the feeling of a complete person behind the word, she repeated, "No."

Sam's mother looked on, piqued. I imagined that the scholar in her was curious to see how I would handle a tough challenge. Sam, I was made to feel, would not do such things.

The forced politeness of the situation was a python squeezing the air out of me. I had to keep up the social chatter while I burned with a caustic compound of shame and anger.

I tried a brief stage of cajoling, just enough to allow me to consider my options. Cajoling is rarely a successful mothering tactic and always humiliating. Assuming a posture of supplication, the large person shrinks before the child. Stature is not easily regained. Nor can one with aesthetic pleasure look on a parent who begs in a desperate, high whine. This much I knew, and vowed to avoid the mistake, especially before this older woman who had initiated the play date and had worked out the arrangements with my husband. With a certain noblesse, she had brought in a child to play, like a Pip summoned to Estella in *Great Expectations*. It was a command performance, really, and my mothering was under unusual audience scrutiny. As a first-timer, I believed the whole globe stopped to watch every time my daughter challenged my authority, while the voice of the maternal world-soul whispered, *What will she do?* Indeed, I did not know what I would do or should do now. I stood paralyzed while a roundtable of experts assembled in my head to debate the best course of action.

Part of me wanted to get back in the car and go home without her. Part of me wanted to slap the other mother for standing smugly in her own yard with her own son who did not have to be removed from his sandbox against his will. Part of me wanted to become enormously large and strong and simply forklift my daughter out of the sandbox from where she glared at me. Into the car we'd go, never to be seen again in these climes.

After a survey of tactics, I settled on forklift manqué. I attempted to lift her from the sandbox so as to set her on her feet in the grass. Since I was not enormously large and strong, however, and lacked all conviction, she writhed out of my grip and bolted with stunning speed out the back gate and into the alley, running with resolute abandon toward the cross street. I hurried after her in maternal terror. Before I could overtake her, she reached the street. If a car had been passing, I could not have prevented her from dashing in front of it. This is a crucial point. Let me repeat. I would have failed to save her.

When I did catch up to her, I grabbed her roughly, swung her over my shoulder, and walked back down the alley, where the woman and her son were watching, in their alarm and aversion displaying a marked family resemblance. I pretended to make light of the escapade.

"Oh, my daughter, she's a breakaway," I joked, following up the witticism with a bit of tattered laughter. I walked around the house to the car parked in front; she was still flung over my shoulder. Sam and his mother followed, watching from their impressive set of front steps as I harnessed my child's unwilling body into her car seat.

I drove two blocks, pulled over to the side of the street, and wept.

Thus was the essential dynamic revealed: I could not make my daughter do what she did not want to do. She possessed more raw and undivided stubbornness than I possessed power to conform her will to mine. Further, the mother-daughter drama would not be private, but would be played out on a vast public stage.

If I could paint this drama, a rendering of my imagination, it would be nothing cold or impersonal, abstract or cubist, but a style in which emotions are expressed sculpturally, as in *Christina's World* by Wyeth. The painting would capture the distance between mother and child, the space at the heart of their bond, a depth no one can fathom and no one can bridge. This field of tension would define mother and child, more important than either of them individually. Let's look at this canvas. She and I are fields of force, pushing and pulling against each other across its space. All else is cut away, even Sam and the mother whose home it was. The sequence that led to pursuit, and all that followed, are external to the tableau of the defining moment. The viewer's eye is drawn first to the daughter, who strives toward the cross street at the end of the alley, her head flung back to see how she is pursued, and then to the mother, lunging out of the backyard gate into the darkening alley, her stricken face in profile, a Gothic convergence of weights and strains upon a slender pier. The angle of view is raised a little from the pavement, close to this alleyed world and gaining a purchase. The painting merges to a single field, with two poles of pursuit and flight, of mother and daughter, of she and I, forever panting and forever young, respectively, as Keats would put it, and forever with the space between.

The Peaceable Kingdom

Mother is the most powerful word in the English language, I think. Mention *mother* and my hidden nerve leaps in a dance of sensation and memory. My mother's face in youth, pictured in photographs, was a face to launch a fleet of ships, a face I wanted to see emerge from a wall of fog, a face I wanted to hang my life on. But by middle age my mother's face was stern and disapproving, and one look sent me whimpering to my room. Fear and beauty, beauty and fear: mother.

This has been a long and clutching story in my family. My mother had a mother and her mother a mother before her, and none of us wanted to be like her own mother.

When my daughter was very young and trusting, she thought I was something I wasn't. She thought I was a mother, first, last, and in between, for the role of mother swallows the woman—from the daughter's point of view. She just assumed I was her mother because she found me in the house sleeping next to her father in the marital bed. Why would I be in the bed next to her father if I wasn't her mother? She assumed I was her mother because I told her I was and she took me at my word. She did not question who I was. She did not search my face for resemblances to hers. From time to time she may have dimly sensed that something I was doing or saying didn't fit the mothering she saw elsewhere, but she did not question what a mother was, and the moment of doubt lifted off as quickly as storm clouds dissipate in a southern sky.

But later she changed. And I wasn't prepared. She started watching me, trying to get at who I was. She started to sense that I was not born a mother, was not a natural-born mother, and that I was not always as she found me. She sensed there was something else about me, some non-mother past underneath the mother topcoat. She started measuring me against other mothers and saw to her displeasure that there was more to me than a mother. At the same time, I began to fail to live up to her measurements of what a mother should be: I was not a creature with wings that doubled as cookie sheets. Previously it hadn't occurred to her that I didn't sew her Halloween costumes like the other mothers on the block, like the mothers she watched on television. I didn't own a sewing machine, or even a needle and thread, standard mother equipment. She noticed that I didn't attend the neighborhood coffees convened on weekday mornings because I worked outside the home. I didn't have a special dish to pass at potlucks because I was a lousy cook, and I wasn't cheerful when hauling out the trash like the other mothers, who waved enthusiastically at each other from their respective curbs.

In elementary school I let her walk home from school even though rumors circulated about an ominous Chevy lingering by the schoolyard. Unlike the other mothers, I wasn't convinced girls had more to fear from strangers than people closer to home. I was not always up when she left for school in the morning. Sometimes I was hung over. Sometimes her father got her ready. Sometimes he even braided her hair. I read books at her soccer games, off to the side of the shouting parents. Often I agreed to bake cookies and then forgot. I felt guilty, but did the exact same thing the next time I was asked. While she sensed the differences between me and other mothers, she didn't question me. The other children didn't question their mothers either. Not yet. The critique of the traffic of mothers hadn't started yet.

By the eighth grade she was openly evaluating my character. She no longer accepted me at face value. Was I consistent, did I contradict myself, did I practice what I preached? Did I have an accurate sense of myself? When I left the house, without announcing my purpose, where did I go, she wondered. Once I became a mother, my previous life became a secret I couldn't reveal. I had to preserve the illusion that I was always as my daughter found me, a born mother who didn't have a life worth mentioning before her daughter arrived. I pretended I had been a good girl, a saint, who never earned a C on my report card or made my mother cry. Sometimes I was on the verge of telling her how difficult I had been at her age, but I didn't.

She did not subject her father to the same scrutiny. He was given a free pass. She regarded me suspiciously and went through my drawers, bags, jacket pockets. She thought that I was someone other than who I seemed, someone who had secrets—because *she* did. That I lived a life other than the one she saw—because *she* did. If she watched me closely enough, I would give myself away. She sniffed me like a bloodhound on a fugitive trail. I increased my vigilance.

When I became a mother, I thought that the watching would be finished, or if not finished, that I would be the one who did the watching. My mother watched me and was unhappy with what she observed. I told myself, when I became a mother, that I would not watch my daughter as my mother had watched me. No eyes would bore into her soul. I would not regard her with suspicion. I would not attempt to enter her every thought, mood, and desire. I would give her privacy. More important than keeping her fed, clothed, and attended to, I would give her a room where she could sit on the bed for dreamy hours, staring out into trees.

Now I feel like my mother, and it frightens me. I recognize in my responses to my daughter my mother's responses to me as I became an adult, a transformation she believed I managed badly. I didn't like how she handled me. I almost want to say manhandled me. And now I am perpetuating that handling upon my daughter. The same tones of accusation ring across the generations, with the same result: my daughter finds me wanting. She compares me to other mothers, who are more understanding, generous, lenient, open-minded, tolerant, and playful. Before this roster of luminaries I am deflated, and I retreat with hurt feelings. I feel strange need of protection around her, as if everything about me is under attack—the way I look, eat, talk, drive. She has an insatiable need to tear me apart, in order to build herself up, just as I needed to protect myself. It is a ritual that must be enacted over and over: to belittle the mother. I offer a wealth of opportunity.

Now I can imagine how my mother felt. She defended herself against me with identifiable strategies. Disengagement: she withdrew her interest and then her affection, which resulted in a brittle and remote demeanor. Preemptive blows: she'd strike before I had a chance to hide or prepare, to put me on the defensive. When those strategies failed, she'd engage in full-scale invasion, as if she were fighting for her life. She erected a hard containing wall of self-righteousness and blamed me for everything that had gone wrong between us. She reconstructed history with supreme creative will.

I recognize all of these techniques in myself. I'm gripped by anxiety because my job is to guide my daughter to adulthood, to keep her on track, to pull her away from the fires of self-destruction. Yet it is her calling to tear up the tracks and ignite the bonfires. I have sometimes flipped into invasion, as my mother before me did. After all my attempts to stand apart from her, my mother lives within me.

Sometimes I think it would be better if mothers and daughters lived in a herd, not a house, and were at an early age turned out to pasture with other mothers and daughters, and that over the course of a few seasons daughters wouldn't know who exactly had borne them, and mothers wouldn't know who exactly they had given birth to, and no one would know whose head she was butting up against, whose call she was following or not following, that there was more than enough of everything to go around, and that the only thing devoured was a deep-green gathering of grass.

Toy Savannah

It is late summer, and my daughter is leaving home to live on her own. She is my first child, and she is vacating the premises she and I have called home for nineteen years. This is an old story, even a cliché. Right now the newspapers are full of such stories. There is an article listing five easy strategies to cope with the "change"; the article avoids the word *loss* as dentists do *pain*. Turn this departure, the author advises, into an opportunity for renewal and adventure. Okay, here is my story of adventure and renewal.

We have not been getting along for the months she has been living at home since her return from Europe, where she traveled for half a year after graduating from high school. We have pretty well torn up the feelings between us and settled into bitter silence, with scattered arguments and patches of wrath.

Arguing over what, you might ask. You know, the usual stuff, like treating our home like a hotel and I'm maid service and cook ("At the Four Seasons," I tell her, "at least you get *tips*"). Never putting gas in the car or cleaning out the paper cups and candy wrappers that litter every trip. Coming in at four in the morning or not at all. Playing loud Phish and Grateful Dead over and over. Receiving thirty-five phone calls a day from friends who expect me to take accurate messages. Being generally rude, hostile, and unhelpful. Calling me out when I ask her to clean her room after the wreckage spills into the hall, making passage to my study treacherous. Announcing she has decided not to attend college and instead plans to move in with three boys, waitressing until she saves enough money to follow Phish on next summer's concert tour.

We have both counted the hours in anticipation of her departure. She says, "Well, you won't have to deal with me much longer. I'm moving out in a month," or in two weeks, or in ten days—you get the idea. And I taunt right back—"Yes, and it can't come a moment too soon." My anger burns so brightly it dims all the stars in my firmament of love.

She packs for days, throwing out bags and bags of what she has accumulated in her nineteen years. She drives off to the Public Works Department with a load of waste and comes back with some piece of furniture she found on a curb. Our garage is a sad collection of ripped and broken chairs and couches, all in a mustard color. Assembling the furniture of her new life, she is feverish with excitement. She even finds a Grateful Dead wastepaper can at one of the garage sales she prowls.

It is Saturday morning, a lovely day with a sun of beaming hope, and Clare is carrying boxes down from her room, loading them into the van, and driving off to her new residence. I feel everything rise that I have pushed aside, pushed down, and pushed under. While she and her brother deliver a load, I visit her room. The drawers of her desk, formerly so full they wouldn't close, sit open and clean; her closet rattles with empty hangers. I can see the floor for the first time in months. The walls are bare except for the picture hooks. The rugs are packed. The bed that I slept upon until I left home, the bed that I passed on to Clare and upon which she slept until now, is stripped of its comforter and pillows. The room is emptied of life. And not as a child might take a few things away to college. She has dismantled her place. She has gone through her life and thrown out the past. She knows she'll never be back. This will never be her primary residence again, the place she calls home.

She will never sleep on that bed again. She is going to make another home for herself, on her own terms. I have not allowed myself to see that she is making the end of childhood.

If I had confronted her departure in stages, I would have been devastated by increments. Now that my anger is abated, I find an empty room and a departed daughter, and a sheet of glass shatters.

The story continues thus: this is what I did with my opportunity for renewal and change. I sat down in a chair and wept until my eyes hurt. I poured myself a shot of vodka. And then I started to clean. Not her room. I wasn't ready to clean her room. I started cleaning the kitchen, the parts I clean only in desperation—the oven, the refrigerator, the sticky blinds on the windows, the cabinet shelves, the legs of the kitchen table. Then I poured myself another shot of vodka, this one larger, grasped my Formula 409 cleaning spray, sat down at the kitchen table, and sobbed.

I contemplated the filth under the table, but instead made a key decision to tear off the old shelf paper and replace it with clean paper I had bought some time ago on sale. Even in the best of times, measuring is something I don't do. Even when I'm sober, patterns are like maps of madness for me. But here I was with my half-drained bottle of vodka, eyes mere slits of weeping, trying to put down shelf paper. My son walked into the kitchen on his way to a bowl of ice cream and said, "Oh no." I had gotten the first sheet of paper folded in on itself and stuck to me. In shape it did not resemble the drawer it was supposed to fit. Taking pity, he unglued me from the paper. "I don't think you should be doing this right now," he said gently. Nonetheless, I struggled forward and managed to lay paper on a few shelves and in one drawer. The paper had ripples, not the smooth fit advocated in the instructions, and ran up jaggedly the sides of the drawer and over the front lips of the shelves.

I contemplate the cabinets and drawers and say, *mothers and daughters . . .*

Two weeks after her departure, I am inside Barnes and Noble, waiting in line to pay for my books. I look out the window. There she is—the tallest of three girls walking away down the street. She was always the tall one emerging at the end of the school day, a giraffe in a toy savannah. The other two girls have their hair pulled back in buns. She alone wears her hair loose and wild.

I pay my bill in a hurry and go out onto the street. They are striding forward with purpose, moving farther and farther ahead, too far for me to catch up. Clare can't hear me as I call after her. Will she look back over her shoulder, I wonder. Not today, I think. The street traffic streams past in a continuous wash while I stand rooted to the sidewalk, unable to step backward or forward.

At first—in the store—I hadn't recognized her. She was just a girl walking with other girls. By the time I saw it was my Clare, she was gone.

STUDIO OF THE VOICE

Studio of the Voice

1. It starts as a muffled cry.

2. Down a long hallway into a wood-paneled room with a wall of windows against which branches slap in a howling wind.

3. No one hears it.

4. It builds and builds and then it eventually dies.

5. "You're the least important person in the room and don't you forget it," Jessica Mitford's governess would hiss in her ear on the advent of any social occasion.

6. Joan Didion copied that into her notebook and it wasn't until late in her career that she was able to enter a room "without hearing some such phrase" in her inner ear.

7. Think of Jane Eyre pitted against the insufferable foe-like Mrs. Reed and her bullying children. After Jane's altercation with John Reed, Mrs. Reed sweeps into the nursery, "crushes" her on the edge of her crib and tells her not to "utter one syllable" for the remainder of the day.

8. After reading one of my poems aloud in college, a female teacher said, "My dear, you have two voices, one tentative and one too fast, and both are a misery."

9. Teachers talked about the voice as if it was disembodied.

10. Yet, I instinctually knew it emanated from my person and my person had a body, in which there were two girls—one who was trapped and feared she had no voice at all, and another who wanted to shout out and make a rumpus.

11. The injunction to remain silent incites Jane, and she is compelled to speak regardless of the consequences. "It seemed as if my tongue pronounced words without my will . . . something spoke out of me over which I had no control."

12. It can't be taught.

13. "The voice is a wild thing. It can't be bred in captivity."—Willa Cather

14. "I'm a very bad subject person," Jamaica Kincaid said.

15. A subject person is a person at the mercy of others—like Jessica and her governess, like Jane and Mrs. Reed, like me and my first-grade teacher Mrs. Joy who commanded the class to be silent. "Silence," she'd say, ruling it to be so. Breaking us to attain it.

16. My mother sent me to school in first grade outfitted in a fancy white dress. At recess I climbed the monkey bars and hung upside down even though I had been told not to. The shiny

white dress flew over my face and Bruce Wray taunted me with *I can see your underpants, I can see your underpants.* I jumped down from the bars and punched him in the stomach. A crowd gathered and in the skirmish Mrs. Joy materialized and marched me back to the classroom whereupon my mother was called. The teacher told me not to say a word, but like Jane I could not be silent, and she put tape across my mouth. When my mother arrived and saw my torn dress and my mouth covered, she smiled at Mrs. Joy and said, "Yes, that's the appropriate response."

17. I came to believe a large body was a prerequisite for vocal power and concluded that the disappointment in my voice was tied to my body. I wasn't tall enough, large enough. I simply wasn't *enough.*

18. I wasn't silent exactly. I spoke but I spoke in such a way that I didn't speak. My voice fell backward onto itself and sounded as if I was speaking from the bottom of a deep well.

19. I swallowed my voice.

20. "I thought how unpleasant it is to be locked out; and then I thought how it is worse perhaps to be locked in."—Virginia Woolf

21. The most remarkable voice I encountered in the studio of the voice was the poet Richard Hugo, not uncoincidentally a large man. His voice could hold multitudes.

22. On my walk home in the chill autumn night, with the sidewalks skirted in fallen leaves, I cursed Richard Hugo, and then I cursed myself. I might as well have a raised a fist to the moon hanging ponderously in the pitch-black sky for all the good it did.

23. How did he *get* that voice? Was it something he ate? Did people listen to him with attention from a very young age? Or was he born with it?

24. I envied his voice for I was tired of being told to speak up, we can barely hear you.

25. I felt such a sense of constriction, of lack.

26. My voice—*I*—was anonymous, bare as workshop walls. The poems I wrote in school, under the schoolmaster's gaze, shrank smaller—a little box, a sentence, a word, a letter, a blank space where the poem—the person—was supposed to be.

27. Of course, I was listening in all the wrong places. If I had been listening to Charlotte Brontë, Virginia Woolf, or Jamaica Kincaid, they might have told me my voice was better than it

sounded to those teachers, even if it would take most of my life to realize it.

28. Years passed. And then one spring day I put my incredible shrinking poems away. I said, "I'm putting you away," and buried them.

29. An hour later out popped the letter *P*.

30. An explosion.

31. *Posture.* My posture, women's posture.

32. Who knew I had so much to say on the subject of my bodily history. Until that moment I was unaware I had feelings, passionate feelings, about my standing, about the alignment of my back and neck and head. Or how much I hated being badgered to *stand up straight* all my life.

33. I wasn't straight at all. That was the thing. I was rounded, curved.

34. Forces had been percolating for years that I had stuffed down and locked away. That afternoon in the third-floor attic of my house the words were released and the rock wedged into the mouth of the cave rolled away.

35. "I consider anger a badge of honor. I've really come to love anger. When people say you are charming you are in deep trouble."—Jamaica Kincaid

36. Here's to you, old voice, cry muffled and unmuffled, unfathomable to your core, connected in countless fucked-up ways to the history of being born, but somehow *in* the pine and the redwood smashing against the windows in that dismal workshop of a nursery and the patch of earth at the back corner of the yard of your childhood where I took my dolls and buried them, in the muscled flank of the horse of ingenuity that I rode when I first felt my voice like blood rushing through me—*I love, I hate, I suffer, I am.*

The Blue Dress

The dress is more of a wound than a dress. After two babies I can't pour myself into it as I once did, and that does not make me sad—just the opposite; it makes me glad. I'm glad that I can't hike the zipper up my back or fasten the tiny buttons in the cinched waist. Now if I tried to step into it, I would rip the fabric apart, tear it, split it, rend it to tatters and that would be a good thing, a very good thing for then I would see that in the blue dress I looked like someone drowning in a mirror.

Odd then, given my feelings about the dress, that I still have it. Usually I want to rid myself of reminders of troubling times, do everything I can to forget, become an amnesiac. I haven't kept the letters a man wrote me who I once loved. When he ended the affair, I threw away every word he had written, every trace of his presence in my life. With great solemnity I carried my bundle of him to the garage, lifted the enormous lid of the dumpster and threw it in with all the force I could muster. I wanted to put him behind me as completely and cleanly as I could—out of sight, out of mind. Little did I think then how those words had been learned by heart and would not be so easy to forget. In the subsequent days before the trash was picked up, my resolve did not weaken. There was no pawing through the garbage in the middle of the night trying to retrieve what I had cast behind me. The blue dress has met a different fate. Even though I never wear it, I've held onto it all these years, and visit it periodically like an invitation to the blues.

My house has no basement, no crawl space, no subterranean caverns but it does have an attic whose eaves slant wickedly. You can't stand all the way up without hitting your head. Sometimes the dress calls to me in the late afternoon when I feel shaky. Instead of taking a shot of whiskey and feeling the burn slide down my throat, I visit the dress. As if undertaking a pilgrimage, I ascend a narrow stairway whose entrance is in my daughter's bedroom on the second floor of our house far, far away from where I bought the dress. The stairs are usually clogged with sleeping bags, summer fans, folding chairs, Christmas decorations and other seasonal items that have never quite reached the summit. Besides seasonal items, the attic is the spot where I deposit all the things I do not use but can't get rid of, relics of a past life and the feelings they provoke—jammed into boxes that block passage to the small closet on the far wall whose single light is burned out. Here is where the blue dress hangs.

I bought the dress the summer of the blackout, of 104 degrees, the second summer of the Son of Sam. I was young then and almost two years divorced from my college professor who I had met the fall of my sophomore year, married, and then divorced by the time I was a senior. To the best of my knowledge I was the only married student at Pomona, and then, a year later, the only divorced one. Quite an education—that—not the one I was expecting or prepared for and afterward I spun my wheels. I had no long-range plans, no sense of where I was going. I had moved from my father's house to my husband's house and had not learned the first thing about standing on my own. I was just trying to stay upright, pay the bills, if barely, and avoid emotional entanglements that might shatter me. After a year of working as a paralegal in a law firm in Philadelphia, a job I thought of as tiding me over until my real work began whatever that was, I accepted an offer to work in their Manhattan office. It had become routine for me to visit one of my best friends from college, who lived in Greenwich Village while finishing her master's at NYU, and so when I got this job offer we decided I would move into her one-bedroom apartment on the top floor of the thirteen-story building with a collapsed ceiling and a serious cockroach problem. At the end of the summer Marian was moving to Boston to begin her doctoral studies at Harvard and I would take over her lease. That was the plan.

I should have known what I was getting into—after all, I had opened the cabinets in her apartment many times and found the hard-shelled bodies, surprisingly long and wide, scurrying to find another port in the storm. I had been accosted on the streets and subways by panhandlers, leered at by men following me too closely. It wasn't as if this was the first time I felt like female prey. No, in my short life I had accumulated a long history as the preyed upon. But somehow the experiences were muted by my friend Marian who would grab my elbow and steer me in and out and away from the hands that sought to touch me. She walked with an attitude that said *Don't mess with me* and remarkably no one did. She even frightened me a little bit. I let her guide me through the city.

I didn't have my bearings but I didn't know that then. On the basis of a few weekend visits I thought that I could handle the city. You'd think my romantic expectations would be held in check or seen as the schoolgirl rubbish they were. I thought I was putting all the disappointments of the past few years behind me and starting fresh in a city I had never lived in. Like a young boy heading west, I fantasized about starting over, erasing my mistakes, and somehow getting back to where I thought I should have been—a young, single woman just starting life on her own. I pictured myself walking along Fifth Avenue with a spring in my step, and later I'd serve cocktails in my small but attractive apartment. I did not lay my marital history on the table—it was information I did not freely provide. When upon occasion my marital status did slip out, it provoked disbelief and wonder and I felt I had to provide an explanation. The story of my life, or some version of it, would be necessary to explain how I had gotten myself into this mess of a marriage and why I got out so quickly. At the time it wasn't a story I was prepared or able to tell. I didn't understand it myself—it was a bafflement, a mistake, a failure, a wound. In my hazy fantasy of moving to Manhattan it never occurred to me that Marian would have her own life, and that instead of her handing me my new life all tied up with ribbons and bows, I would have to make one of my own.

The day in June when I moved in, it was as if I was seeing the building for the first time. It was remarkably derelict. Riding the elevator up to the thirteenth floor, I noticed a sign taped to the wall, and shifting the box I was carrying to my left hip, I leaned in to read:

> BEWARE. Rapist
> Disguised As A Plumber
> On Your Block

Underneath the bold caption, a brief description of how the rapist gained access to the women's apartments: he said the landlord sent him and the doors opened. Was the sign new, I wondered, or had I never noticed it before? It had to be a mistake or a prank. The ominous warning was so out of keeping with what I wanted, with what I had moved to New York City for. That was the first sign that my move might have been a mistake, but because so much was riding on this fresh start, I chose to deflect my fear and respond with false bravado.

To Marian I said, "If our apartment's problems are typical, I can see how the doors might fly open to anyone claiming the landlord sent them."

Marian didn't laugh, but then she had lived on the thirteenth floor in the apartment for two years before I arrived and had long stopped pretending to be brave. She had watched as the ceiling in the bedroom split open and sank low, and no one in management did a thing despite her repeated calls.

In the weeks of moving in and starting my job, the truer picture of New York City and my life in it emerged. Each morning I encountered exactly no one in the small hall on my floor, not a door opened or closed in my presence. I'd notice a bag of overflowing trash outside an apartment and the accompanying cockroaches but never see who the trash belonged to. Not a word, not a deed, not a hello not a goodbye, not a smile, not even a face, and certainly no names were exchanged as I rode the elevator down to the ground floor and walked by the mailboxes before I exited the building onto Eleventh. If I required assistance, it was hard to believe anyone would emerge to help me. Who would come—ghosts? No sooner would the building's door slam shut when the gusts of hot dirty air hit me. The city was experiencing a brutal heat wave dripping with humidity. The grit would settle on my face and I'd wonder why I bothered to wash it. I'd take a sharp left and walk to the bus on Fifth Avenue, picking my way around mounds of white bags of trash the size of small whales sprawled across the sidewalks and spilling into the streets because there was now a garbage strike. I had to be careful not to trip over the legs of homeless men braced against the walls of buildings in makeshift abodes. Without Marian, hands touched me, sometimes tugging at my purse, lips were wetted. I took the bus on Fifth to my upscale place of work—the Steuben Glass Building on Fifty-Seventh near Central Park where I was not a lawyer and not a secretary but the only paralegal, neither fish nor fowl, in the heart of stores too expensive for me to even enter. I couldn't find a place cheap enough to buy lunch. No heaps of trash bags overflowed upon the streets in this commercial district and I wondered what they did with the trash in midtown to make it disappear. And the homeless, where did they go? Here for a few blocks I could walk unimpeded. I took the elevator to the seventh floor and the leverage bonds department of the excessively air conditioned law firm and began collating documents in my cubicle. Ah romance!

To no one's surprise but my own, the single life wasn't measuring up to what I had imagined. Instead of taking one step forward, I was taking two steps back. Instead of building a life, I was unraveling the thin one I had. Work and home were lonely and in between a combat zone. Neither the lawyers nor the secretaries claimed me as one of them and I was never included in lunch plans or drinks after work. The work itself was more tedious than the tedious work I had done in Philadelphia because it was not enlivened by companionship. In the Philadelphia firm I shared an office with another paralegal and even if we had to keep track of our time in six-minute increments straight out of Kafka, at least we could escape for lunch and drinks at the end of the week. Marian was more absent than present, visiting her family on the Cape for weeks at a time and finishing her thesis.

To escape the leverage bonds and the trash bags and the dripping water from the hole in the ceiling and the wreckage I thought I had left behind and the loneliness, I went shopping by myself in the Village one humid Saturday afternoon. In the midst of the still hippie kingdom I stumbled upon a little retro store full of dresses that might have been specially made for Marilyn Monroe. I can't remember which movie of hers the store was named after—*Some Like It Hot* (which would have been appropriate) or *Seven Year Itch*. An electric blue skin the color of the morpho butterfly, iridescent in flight, spoke to me from its jammed place on the rack. I disentangled it and draped it over my arm carefully and moved into the makeshift changing room behind a drawn velvet curtain. It reminded me of the fuchsia dress Marilyn memorably wore like dagger and sheath in *Niagara*, a noir movie in color made before I was born about a marriage drowning at the falls and the only movie in which Marilyn died—her husband strangled her to death—though I didn't remember that then. I should have considered her unsavory end, how her slender neck was no match for her husband's powerful hands, before pulling the dress off the hanger. But instead I remembered the way men watched her walk. How the camera was in thrall to her sashaying in her high heels like a bell swinging back and forth. My dress was a mid-calf, love-cut dazzler made of clingy stretch material like silk jersey. A zipper ran from the buttocks to the midpoint of my back, where the material ended. I had to pour myself into the dress. To say the dress was fitted doesn't begin to get at its shape or the shape I assumed once I bled into it.

When I emerged from behind the dusky curtain to look at myself in the store's one full-length mirror an older saleswoman wearing a flounced gypsy costume in shades of purple with large hoop earrings nodded approval. She shook her arm covered with silver bangles for emphasis. *You were built for another time,* she said, *a time of curves.* She said I might do some damage in that dress, and we laughed together. I threw back my head and it felt good. I hadn't laughed with anyone since I had moved to the city. I bought the dress even though I couldn't afford it and doubted I would wear it. It was one thing to try the dress on in a retro fantasy, but it was inappropriate for my workplace—it was trouble. The dress would likely hang in my closet where I would visit it and brush its sheeny bodice across my cheek.

But I did wear the dress that summer. Not right away. After the blackout in mid-July, something broke in me. I felt I had to do something and I pulled the dress from its hanger and slithered into it. The night of the blackout I had spent by myself curled up in the armchair by the window looking out on all the dark windows in the apartment buildings across the way and listening to the sirens that never stopped wailing. The city had boiled over. Looting, arson, fear, and anger. When the power came back on and I returned to work, I wore the dress with high-heel strappy sandals that were just as impractical as the dress to navigate my way along the pocked sidewalks. I now understood why Marilyn Monroe walked as slowly as she did. The dress was so tight that it required all my ingenuity to get up onto the bus—I had to hike the hem a few inches and turn sideways to achieve the necessary spread to mount that first step. I made a spectacle of myself getting on the bus and I liked it, at least I thought I did. I thought it was better to make a spectacle of myself rather than continue trying unsuccessfully to blend in. The dress brought me attention from all manner of men. Starting off my dull workday became exciting—cab drivers, cab passengers, panhandlers, men on their way to work, men walking dogs noticed me. I was whistled at, greeted by crude salutations and shouts of raw appreciation. Even the male lawyers noticed me for the first time. I experienced the gamut of male response and felt I was the still center around which men pivoted and I felt hard and powerful.

And angry.

I wouldn't have been able to say why I felt angry then or even that it was anger acting in me. I didn't know what I saw in the shape and color of the dress, why I pulled it off the hanger or why I felt I belonged inside it. I didn't realize that the blue dress, tight like a bottle, was shaped like my anger. But I was angry, a desperate, free-ranging, impotent kind of anger that swung from one thing to another. I was angry at the way my father controlled my mother, my sisters, and me, how he plotted our lives, was the moneymaker and the dispenser of our allowances, he could say yes or he could say no, he could throw money in my face as he had or lock me in my bedroom until I was subdued. I remembered how when our neighbor had paid me for taking care of her horse for a week; my father didn't believe me when I said I didn't ask to be paid, that Mrs. Collingwood had forced the ten dollars into my hand. I had given the money to my father as he had asked and he had torn the bill into little pieces and thrown them in the air in my direction. And then, of course, I had run into my room and refused to come out for dinner. I was angry that my father made me go to a prom with the son of one of his associates even when I didn't want to and knew the guy was seriously weird and aggressive. I was angry that my father never apologized when that same boy shot up our mailbox when he believed I slighted him. I had a whole laundry list of men I was angry with—the eighth grade science teacher who paddled me in front of the class because I jittered my legs while seated in my chair, and angry at the boys in fifth grade who stole my crutches when I broke my leg and locked me in the library closet and took turns kissing me, and all the boys who over the years thought they could put their hands on my breasts whenever they felt like it. I was angry that my father never stopped the marriage he was aghast at and knew was a disaster. And what about my professor who picked me up, drank me, and then threw me to the ground? If I had known that the blue of the dress I bought was the blue of the male morpho butterfly, not the female, I would have been angry about that too.

I was angry at so many instances of feeling powerless before some man starting so far back I couldn't even name all that I was angry about. And I was especially angry that a man posing as a plumber was terrorizing my block. I was angry that finally I was supposed to be charting my own independent course but I was afraid to go to a bookstore or a movie by myself at night and come out into the dark. Angry that I felt vulnerable standing under a streetlight, waiting at a bus stop, entering a subway station. I was angry that I was sitting by myself in my thirteenth-story apartment with the ceiling dripping and listening to the cockroaches moving through their dark passageways, going over and over all the mistakes I had made and couldn't be unmade. I was filled with stinking rage and I couldn't do a thing about it but get in that blue dress and make the men I walked by want me. I wanted to attract men and then toy with them the way I had been toyed with. I never wanted a man's hands to wrap around my tiny waist and I never reached out my arms to bring a man closer. When I wore the blue dress I was not looking for the warmth of touch. I didn't complain about the crudeness of the catcalls. I felt alive, the blood rushing to my cheeks. I felt my breasts swell under the tight binding, the curve of my calves stabbed me, I felt myself walking and mounting the steps, I felt myself getting up and sitting down. I had never been so aware of myself. The blue dress was creating me and carrying me forward, or so I believed.

I did not see then, but I was like the red-bellied woodpecker that flew into the glass when I was eleven. She used the tree outside the window as her launching pad. She started sideways, at an angle from the tree, and flew full speed ahead, without hesitation, directly at the window. She was deranged in some way I couldn't understand. Her pointed beak and red belly thumped against the glass and then she'd right herself and begin the process again. I expected to find her body in one of the planters. I couldn't believe she'd remain undeterred. I opened the glass door and ran outside, waving my arms to shoo her away. I sprayed water at her, hung purple towels from the railings. I tried everything I could to stop her and failed. She'd momentarily swerve away from the window and then come right back. Much later someone explained that she saw a rival in the glass and wanted to obliterate the sight. But then I thought she was pounding her own image to relieve herself of it. Still part of me believes she was turning on herself. And then the spell of madness was over. She was gone. The windows were covered with milky white trails, squiggles and claw marks, thick deposits where her beak landed, but she never broke through and she never fell into the planters.

By the end of the summer, when the temperature finally dropped, the police caught Sam and the sign about risky plumbers got layered over and it was done. Marian moved to Boston, but I did not take over her lease. My sojourn on the thirteenth floor under the ceiling with a hole to the sky was over. Nor did I continue in the leverage lease department in the Steuben Glass Building. The summer of the blue dress was over. I never wore the dress again. Nevertheless when I moved to Los Angeles I took the blue dress with me, carried it all the way across the country. Two years later, my apartment was robbed—the thief had cleaned me out, including almost all my clothes except for the blue dress. Did he see its impossible fit, the contortions that were required to fit oneself to the dress, and leave it behind? It has since followed me wherever I have gone, up the coast to Seattle and then across the country again to Michigan.

And I keep it still, though the dress is not what it once was. Hard to believe it ever held a blue sheen electric enough to make me think of the iridescent flight of the blue morpho butterfly. That sheen is faded from years of sunlight coming in from the lone window in the attic. To think I once felt powerful in its ruins. I never pull the dress off its hanger and hold it against my body. I never inhale its scent deeply and wish I could return to those days when I was willing to bleed to wear it.

Bree Daniels

She sits in a small, dark office, facing her matronly psychiatrist, whose gray hair snakes up into an old-fashioned bun. Children's drawings brighten the wall behind her, pastel skies, red houses, a nuclear stick family standing in front. For the moment she's insulated from the rush of traffic outside and the filth of Manhattan, the piles of garbage spilling into the streets. She doesn't take off her sleek brown jacket, worn over a cream-colored turtleneck. She isn't staying long and doesn't want to get too comfortable. Or she can't get comfortable. Her chestnut hair is cut asymmetrically and hugs her beautiful small head, almost like a helmet, both masculine and feminine, famously called a shag, the perfect name for its ragged modernism.

She looks a little unhinged, untamable. No one would mistake her for a wife. How tense and restless she is, tightly wrapped, coiled, unhappy to stay still in her chair. She's like a racehorse or a tiger pacing in a cage, a lean and wary animal who senses threats on her skin. She could spring out of her chair and strike without hesitation, maybe regretting it later.

She's Bree Daniels, who has left whatever small town to come to New York to become an actress. She's played by Jane Fonda in the 1971 neo-noir crime thriller *Klute*. If I were asked which character I feel closest to in film, I would say Bree Daniels. She isn't the most likable and she certainly isn't helpful. Some would say she is her own worst enemy. She's mixed-up, hanging onto some core of herself by the skin of her teeth. But she is so very alive.

Bree finds herself in a tangle, and not for the first time. That's what you get when your career plans haven't panned out and you turn to prostitution to keep afloat. She's always one step away from disaster. And in this moment the threats are very real: an out-of-town man whom she hooked up with some months back has mysteriously disappeared and his policeman friend, John Klute, has been hired to investigate. The man is dead, it turns out, killed by another Bree client, a violent man she can't remember who is stalking her.

Alan J. Pakula, the director, described the movie as "a melodrama in which a girl's tragic flaw nearly destroys her." Like

Oedipus, the underthinker. Like Hamlet, the overthinker. In the heart of their strength is their weakness. Flawed Bree needs to feel that she is in control. Bree is the overcontroller.

Control—who's got it and who doesn't—that's what *Klute* is about. Control isn't an issue for Bree alone. The main characters—the killer, the policeman, the actress/prostitute—all wear masks of control that turn out to be impossible to wear. The mask slips away and what's underneath is exposed. On the surface Bree appears competent, resilient, tough. She walks with confidence and purpose. In her dealings with clients, she is relaxed and masterful—the performance of seduction and pleasure is a role she knows cold. It's a part she can breathe in. In fact, it's more than that—when her life falters, when she's passed over in an audition, she returns to tricking, like a fix, an addiction. It isn't just a need to make money—Bree regains her equilibrium by showing that she is good at something, that she can control a game rather than be played as a pawn. "For an hour I'm the best actress in the world," she says, "the best fuck in the world."

Bree's therapy sessions, largely improvised by Fonda, are sprinkled throughout the film. In these scenes the camera remains fixed on her in medium close-up, occasionally cutting to her therapist. In this closeted space with the children's paintings behind her, Bree's true feelings come out. She stops performing her confident, in-control self. Her voice changes. Outside of therapy, with her tricks, Bree's voice is low, well-modulated, hard even. When she answers the phone, which she does repeatedly, and says *Bree Daniels,* her voice is dark and throaty and rich—masterful. Fonda says that her voice in *Klute* emerged because she was coming into her own as a woman; others say it came from her bulimia. Whatever the cause, her voice in *Klute* is commanding.

The killer listens to her voice compulsively on a tape he has procured. He even suggests that her voice coaxing him to let it all hang out has set this tragedy in motion. Her voice is colored by contempt for men, by her mastery of them. She leads men where she wants them to go. But the voice in therapy, speaking to another woman, is higher pitched—it rises and falls with the emotions that animate it, her confusion and anger, her frustration with the shrink who can't help her quit tricking. Her hands gesture along with her voice, rising and falling, and a childlike helplessness gets acted out when they fold under her chin.

I know a thing or two about voice. People used to say my voice was so polished, smooth, and pleasant, that I could make a living selling it. I didn't know what they were talking about. The voice I heard was young, unsure, and without force—it betrayed me.

I know a thing or two about control, too. Life can seem like one big audition in which we subject ourselves to all manner of degradation and certain rejection. Will we be chosen for the role, the job, the opening, for love? Bree's vulnerable because she wants parts but she can't control the outcome, and that undoes her and spins her back to doing tricks. There she always gets the role. After humiliating failure in a casting call, she walks straight to a pay phone and lines up a trick *right away*, like a junkie calling her dealer.

Her psychiatrist asks whether Bree enjoys the sex. She answers no. Her psychiatrist wants to know why Bree isn't getting parts. "What's the difference between going out on a call as a model or an actress and a call girl? You're successful as a call girl." Bree interrupts: "When you're a call girl, you control it. That's why."

Days into the investigation, after Klute has shown his disgust with the way she lives, Bree visits him in the little room where he's been staying. She seduces him. It's easy. It's a retaliation for his judgments of her life and it's a recalibration of relative power. Seducing him gives Bree the upper hand, something she desperately needs, or so she thinks. In sex he reveals himself to her, gives himself to her, and that makes him vulnerable. "I never come with a john," she says afterward, letting him know he is no more than a mark. But he is more than a mark. She is losing control.

When I was young, I collected boys. It was what I was raised to do. The only thing my parents approved of was my ability to attract boys as my older sisters had done before me. I don't know if my sisters cared a whit for these boys—they came, and they went. I had difficulty caring, I know that. I wasn't like other girls who fell hard for boys. My heart didn't have much to do with my romantic interactions. Being in control did. It was a performance, like Bree performing a trick. I turned myself into what the boys, and later men, wanted. I listened intently to what they had to say, I smiled, I flattered. I was easy, excellent company, never demanding or difficult. I was very seductive. And I gave men just as much as I had to. I reveled for a long time in the exercise of my control and did not mourn the intimacy I didn't have. Real intimacy would require I give up some of my control, a price I wasn't willing or able to pay for a long time.

In one of the later therapy sessions Bree mentions Klute:

"Well, there's this detective. He took care of me."

"Do you feel threatened by it?"

"Well, I don't know. When you're feeling lonely and someone comes in and moves that around, it's kind of scary, I guess."

Ambivalent is too soft a word for what Bree feels about Klute. She tries to destroy what she feels, to derail the relationship. But Klute doesn't scare easily—he hangs in with her, and this is entirely new to Bree. She has never been with someone with whom she felt open. She says, "I enjoy making love with him, which is a baffling and bewildering thing because I've never felt that before." She can't let herself feel. "But all the time I feel the need to destroy it, break it off, to go back to the comfort of being numb again."

Is this the tragic flaw—Bree's compulsion to destroy her own happiness—because she can't control it?

In a scene late in the movie Bree and Klute visit an outdoor market at night. The streets are crowded, and they make their way to the fruit stands, where he selects fruit to put in little brown paper bags. Bree stands behind him watching, as if she has never been shopping with a man before. The most ordinary activity for a couple—shopping for food—is something miraculous for her. She reverts to her dubious self and steals a plum when she thinks Klute isn't watching, but he sees her. She can't quite quit being on the make, and he can't let her get away with it.

He expects more from her than she is accustomed to give. As he feels which apples to choose, she rests her head on his shoulder. She catches herself and shakes her head. She's not used to such tenderness. She gives a little smile, baffled by her own feelings. When they head home from the market, Bree grabs the hem of his jacket. It's the most wonderful, understated love scene and wholly unexpected in this dark movie. She watches his hands testing the apples, the way he drops the fruit into the bag, the easy way he moves among the crowd, at home in the world, making a home for her. She's not quite in this world yet but she holds onto the hem of his jacket and can follow him, which is more than she's ever done before.

In the original screenplay by Andy Lewis, Klute proposes to Bree. Pakula found that ending a bit too much and tempered the optimism with *ambivalence.* There's that word again. The film ends with a voice-over of Bree's last therapy session as she and Klute carry their suitcases through the emptied apartment toward the door. They're leaving New York together.

The phone rings. She hesitates, puts her suitcase down, and walks to the phone. She might undo what she has decided, we think, she might stay, meet an old client. She picks up the phone and answers, "Bree Daniels," in the seductive tones we know. We don't know what she's going to say. Looking at Klute, who stands by the door watching her, she tells the caller she's leaving town and won't be back. She sounds confident, at least for the moment. The call finished, she shrugs, meaning, *What could I do? Old habits die hard.*

The last words come from therapy. In a voice that rises and falls away, turning her around once again, she says, "I have no idea what will happen. Maybe I'll come back. You'll probably see me next week."

Garbo and the Norns

My first post-menopausal medical exam was scheduled in late fall, and I did not look forward to it. Even if the examiners speak in low tones and warm their tools, a pap smear and gynecological assessment are always ignominious. I dreaded the exam room lit by Beckett, the patient—that is, me—supine upon the examination table, belly up and legs wide in the pitiless stirrups. We offer ourselves to the heavens, yet we never spread enough, never achieve full disclosure, and the nurse always exhorts to do more. I dreaded the paper gown with impossible ties in the back that never closes and never properly conceals. In my first gynecological exam thirty-odd years ago, this gown took on more significance than a closet full of prom dresses. It was my only prop against the masculine and gruff Dr. Sieger, who didn't believe in coddling patients, and just ordered me out of my clothes and onto the table.

Now, having passed from pre- to peri- to post-menopausal without a word to a health professional, I knew I would get disapproving questions about my medical care. I hadn't had a period for more than a year. From the time I was twelve until the transition began, I had not missed one, except for my two pregnancies. Even then it returned twenty-six days to the hour after each birth. Regular is what I had been, punctual, as if something had been waiting for the moment, holding back, anxious to begin. Even my PMS had fixed stages, first bloating and moodiness, then an intense need to clean the house, a grouse with my husband, sleepless nights, nausea, cramps—all of this to usher in the blood. A day or two later came the lifting of mood and spirits, the return of a live-and-let-live grace, the emergence of family members from refuges and hiding places. Reliable as the cycle of summer and winter, spring and fall, this was the rhythm of my blood, painful, inconvenient, messy, debilitating, sometimes cursed. Only now that it was gone could I see it as a blessed sign of youth and life.

The word *menopause* has lost something in the course of its evolution—not a pause, but a termination!—and applies best to the first steps. The disappearance was gradual and erratic. My period became irregular, ceasing for a few months and then, following its own mysterious ways, revisiting. For a long time I didn't make much of this new pattern, letting it trickle away into the vast reservoir of phenomena I am too inattentive to notice, prefer not to interpret, or don't know what to do about. For months after its final disappearance, I expected my period to return, like a bear in hibernation or a favorite TV show on summer hiatus. I waited as if for a tempestuous friend at the train station, ready to meet the pain and crimson glory. But now it was gone forever.

Once the process of cessation was finished, I made an appointment to see a doctor, in my usual way of turning the sensible course of things on its head. I am passive about all things medical, and intensely so when it comes to those having to do with sexuality. I grew up during the era of perfect silence on the subject. The sexual revolution never made it to my house. Menstruation, pregnancy, labor, birth, miscarriage, infertility, abortion, menopause, hysterectomy—they happened offstage, behind screens and veils, with whispers across the generations. On these matters my mother declined to speak. When I think of her, I think of a woman who on the subject of reproduction couldn't help me because she couldn't help herself.

She had her hysterectomy when I was in the fourth grade. The conditions that required it must have worsened precipitously, for the procedure was performed after Labor Day, and that Friday my father drove my sister off to college and was gone for the weekend. Father and daughter loaded the station wagon with sweaters and skirts, typewriter and books, stuffed bears and keepsakes and other hopeful appurtenances. Our house, to which we had just moved that summer, sat on a plateau at the top of a hill like the Acropolis, and as the car pulled away and down the long rounding driveway—my sister never to live at home again—my mother lay listless on the chaise longue in the bedroom at the back of the house, with shades drawn across the long row of windows overlooking the woods, wishing not to be disturbed.

When my father and sister had driven away, I walked to the back of the house and entered the still and dark of the bedroom. My mother was reclining, eyes closed, in the new long chair with its stylish cream-and-gold fabric, which she had picked for just that spot and its view of the woods. Her draped eyes and marble posture showed that she wanted nothing, and certainly not my questioning presence. I knew only that she had had an operation, and I asked her what kind of operation she had.

She said, "A female kind of operation."

"You mean ..." I began, unsure where to head next.

"A hysterectomy. My uterus was removed."

I didn't know what either of those two things was, and when I probed a bit more, she spoke of bleeding. Then her eyes dropped again and she waved me from the room with a weak hand, unmoving otherwise, head pillowed, nerveless, dozing, as if she and the chair were carved from the same stone, the sculpture of an exhausted god.

I spent the afternoon riding my bike down the steep driveway as fast as possible. It curled down between two wooded lots, and at the bottom you could go straight and shoot out into the road, or curve right into a blacktopped circle with an old oak growing in the middle, where I turned around to ride back up the hill. Each time I plunged down the driveway, I took more risk. First I'd lift one foot from the pedal, then a hand from the handlebars. Each trip down I upped the ante, until at last I took both hands off the bars, sat upright, closed my eyes, and plunged for the bottom. I opened them just as the world in the form of the oak in the turnaround was coming up fast. I smacked it hard and hit the ground, entangled in my bike. Something was wrong with my right leg. I called for help, but knew that no one would come. Our nearest neighbor lived on a farm a half mile down the road, and my mother was dozing in her shuttered room at the far side of the house.

I left my bike in a heap and hobbled up the hill, entered the house through the garage, climbed the basement steps, and dragged myself into my mother's room, where she lay insensible to the world. When I roused her, she seemed incapable of grasping what had happened. Over the next two days my leg swelled and throbbed, and then Sunday night my father came home and took me to the hospital, where x-rays showed it was broken. This was the plumb sort of thing doctors were good at, and they clapped a cast on and fixed me right up.

And that was my first insight into women's reproductive destiny.

As I entered the medical complex for my menopause exam, the sun was sinking toward the horizon somewhere behind a gray cover of clouds. I found the right office, filled out my forms, and sat. After a spell of waiting, a nurse assistant ushered me into the examination room. She was middle-aged, too, but fighting it tooth (bleached white) and nail (lacquered scarlet). Her role seemed to require that she crisply refuse any kinship with me. Her hair was a true platinum blond, almost white under the clinical lights, and she wore a stylish brown suit with a faux fur collar that coiled about her neck. When did nurses stop wearing anonymous scrubs and sensible shoes? I had avoided the doctor's office so long that whole revolutions in style had occurred. She shoved a paper gown into my hands (that much had not changed), telling me to undress completely and wait for the doctor. I did so, perched on the edge of the wide exam table, clutching the loose ends of my gown and ruminating on the nurse's fur-wrapped throat and cinematic hair.

Like Garbo, I thought. As a young woman, I had watched with intense pleasure the flashing scenes of her classic performances in *Camille* and *Anna Karenina*. In both roles, she died tragically young. This was as it had to be, for it was impossible to imagine a plot that displayed Garbo in later age. Far better to kill her off than have her grow old. She must purchase with death her eternal youth onscreen—that was the logic. In practical terms, she retired from the movies and withdrew from public view before the age of forty. And yet, I recalled, she regretted her retirement and—

There was a single knock on the door and a younger woman entered, pale and thin, the doctor, in her middle thirties, who introduced herself and offered her hand. It was thin and cold, her handshake unconvincing and tense. I wondered what she was nervous about—I was the naked one in a paper outfit. Was she new to this rotation, or did menopausal women put her off? She wouldn't look me in the eye, but glanced wide right, as if searching for a feminine past and future, written on the wall behind me.

"When was your last period?" she asked.

"Maybe a year ago, or longer. It had been intermittent for some time before that."

"Hormone replacement?"

"No."

"No?" Her eyebrows formed quizzical arches. Natural, not waxed, I guessed.

Under questioning, I admitted that, at the time I last saw a doctor, my blood still flowed like wine.

"Are you troubled by anything?" the doctor asked. "Hot flashes, vaginal dryness?"

"Well, no, not generally." Had she asked about feelings of general decline and diminishment, I might have said yes. When I was younger and fertile, I listened to older friends talk about menopause—or the change, as they called it—as if they were describing Nepal, a foreign country I'd never visit. Accounts of flashes and fatigue lodged in my brain, to resurface now in haunting snippets. Had I listened more carefully and asked questions, I might have noticed that these women had read their portion from the table of fate, and been better prepared for what lay ahead.

"Are you sexually active?" Her voice was shaky. She couldn't have been much of a singer, for even her speaking voice couldn't hold pitch.

"Yes."

"Yes?"

From her tone and body language I intuited that women hitting a certain age were expected to renounce the erotic, and swiftly.

While I answered the questions on her checklist, she offered not the smallest token of warmth. I seemed to be an abnormal specimen who fit no protocol. When she got to the bottom of her list, she offered a conclusion, or perhaps it was another question that I could affirm or deny: "You're post-menopausal, then." It sounded like a death sentence. I was wobbling on the banks of the Styx and would shortly fall in.

By now the assistant in the fur collar had returned for the visual inspection, or exam proper, wheeling an enormous cart carrying, so far as I could see, nothing more than a speculum. She was accompanied by another woman, apparently a supervisor, whose purposes were never announced. Four of us were now squeezed into the small room—three huddled in a semicircle about the cart, and me splayed on the table, feet in the stirrups. While the speculum warmed in a towel, the nurse assistant asked me the same series of questions I had just answered for the doctor. After the sexually active question, the three eyed each other in a collective smirk.

That must be the look of the Norns, the Norse fates, I

thought—Urth, Verthandi, and Skuld, who determined the length of life. They lived at the base of the world tree, the navel of the cosmos, but according to the myth, even it withered. The Norns tried to slow the process by pouring mud and water over its branches, and also held the job of carving a woman's destiny into staves of wood. They were imperious writers, no doubt. What could stand against them? Who called them into being, and why? Not even the Norse gods could escape their fate. Not even Garbo.

They were here to determine my allocation of life, and something about my case perplexed them—that I was too young to be post-menopausal? That I was sexually active? That I had passed through the change without expert assistance?

When the speculum was warm, the nurse assistant handed it to the doctor, who inserted it timorously. They stood at the foot of the examining table and looked into my vagina and clucked with dissatisfaction. They must have seen a ruin, showing neither form nor beauty, a dead tree rotted from the inside out. This was the final humiliation. I was done for, of no further use. My body had betrayed me, time had betrayed me, the weird sisters of medical fate had betrayed me.

I was determined to address my doom with fortitude. One can do great things in life lying down—sex, birth, sleep—so I stirred my courage and asked in a timid voice, "What's wrong?"

"We can't see," they said. The walls of my vagina would not spread, and all was dark to their mirror.

She regretted her retirement. That mattered to me. She contemplated a return to film, but no suitable role came available. The public did not want to see a middle-aged Garbo—that was a contradiction in terms. We could not entertain an older beauty who rode triumphantly beyond youth. Better to let her screen portrait live with us forever while the star aged off-screen, behind heavy curtains. No images emerged to erase or embellish those of her arrested youth. We froze her hallowed head in the world's lit doorways and ourselves alone groped along its dark streets. She died at the age of eighty-four, the news accompanied on television by a montage of old clips and stills. Impossible, I thought, leaning back from the screen. Garbo old, Garbo dead? In the long decades of her moratorium, global blocs broke apart and reformed, plagues came, the Himalayas inched upward, the galaxy was reinvented, but no frown ever marred Garbo's perfect brow.

Eventually the speculum did its job, and the three women were able to get a peek through to my cervix. "Ah," they said. They had sighted the roots of life.

I used to dismiss Garbo's gorgeous myth. I was still young at the time of her death, roughly her age when she disappeared from the screen. My son was three years old, my daughter seven. Teeming with health and possibility, I could have more children if I wanted, as an option, a choice, a door that had not been closed, a door that never would swing shut on its own. When we are robust in health, bending easily, we cannot imagine the fragility of illness, how easily we could break, how hard it might be to rise from our bed. When we are young and fertile, when pregnancy is something we guard against, we cannot imagine the sterility of age. We are eternally gorgeous and rich in our temple. But Garbo happens to us all: deep inside, the invisible process of age is in full swing, intimate with our fluttering heart. Infertility comes too soon, before our hair has turned a snowy shawl, sooner than is right or just. Suddenly we are alone, like toppled columns in a sea of softly rounded mothers-to-be. Yet when we look into the mirror, we greet the girl we used to be.

By now the three women and their hissing cart had slithered out of the room. I retracted my feet from the stirrups, reassembled myself, and got my bearings. Signs for the exit, which I followed blindly, pointed down bright empty corridors till I was spun through a turnstile and out into the fresh air.

The skies were filling with black, and the season's first blooms of snow were lilting down to melt upon the downed sepia leaves. O Mother! We fall far from the tree of life, tinged red with a final vibrancy. We toss in descent, breaking into a wild freedom that seems, for a few seconds, eternal. The tree withers, goes bare into the deep snows of winter, prepares for apples or pears in the spring.

I wished I had ridden my bike. I would have liked to hold it boldly upright, plant my foot hard on the pedal, swing my leg over and mount. I would have ridden off with reckless abandon, vision veiled but eyes wide and alive. My heart came up, and I felt a pulsion in my arms and chest. It was good to have the snow on my skin and know, yes, the rhythm of my unrelenting blood.

Marilyn Monroe's Feet

She was thinking that, after all, feet are the most important part of the whole person; women, she said to herself, have been loved for their feet alone.

—Virginia Woolf, "Street Haunting"

I've taken some posters of classic movie stars to be framed at the hobby shop, and have laid a photograph of Marilyn Monroe out on a long blond table to be measured. In it she sits on a wicker chair, black emptiness behind her, and bends toward the camera at an angle that pulls her strapless ballerina dress away from her chest. The tulle of the costume spills out over the arms of the chair. She is pigeon-toed, shoeless, and *en pointe*, her heels lifted off the floor, her weight focused onto her toes.

The clerk who's helping me looks to be retired, picking up a few dollars to supplement his Social Security, and old enough to have experienced Monroe when her moon of fame first rose, now so long ago. As he takes the dimensions with his tape, he says forcefully, "They should have cut off her feet." I see him at a job involving machinery, maybe selling chainsaws at Sears. I don't think he has an artistic eye.

"You don't mean literally," I joke with a nervous laugh, hugging my purse closer. I like her feet. Her toenails are painted the same dark shade as her fingernails and lips, squarish disks of color that draw my eye down to her feet and unify the portrait.

"They should have cropped it at her knees. Or if not at her knees, somewhere on that stretch down to her ankles. Who wants to look at her feet?"

"I love her feet," I interject. "That's my favorite part of the photo."

He looks at me funny, like Lady, this is Marilyn Monroe we're talking about, not some run-of-the-mill dame. You know, the biggest sex symbol in history.

She of the come-hither visage and the plunging cleavage. Though those aren't the words he'd use.

Besides the extra cash, I'll bet he likes getting out of the house, away from his nagging wife, a modern-day Mrs. Van

Winkle, whose crankiness sent her husband Rip scurrying up the mountain.

I want to put my hands on my hips and say, "I'm aware of who Marilyn Monroe is, thank you." But I don't, because I'm grateful for what he didn't say and he's right about what people want to look at in a photo of the famous one. To be honest, my protestations of love don't tell the whole story. I didn't buy the poster because of her feet. I didn't even notice them when I stumbled upon it online. The usual reasons compelled me to this photo—the whole superstructure of Marilyn Monroe's iconic image. I wasn't thinking about the foundation of the structure, her feet. It took some time living with the photo for me to see that her feet demanded my attention.

Most people would look first at Marilyn Monroe's famous face. It's her face that occupies the most forward position in the photograph's plane, the focal point, as if Milton Greene, the photographer, were saying "Look at her face, look at this amazing face, would you."

But when the poster arrived, released from its tight cylinder and unrolled, I realized that while we all do look at her face, we don't see it, not any more. If we lived during her lifetime and while paging through *Life* magazine came upon this photograph, maybe we'd stop and really see it. Now forty-odd years after her death, her face is too famous. We've seen it plastered on coffee cups and T-shirts and greeting cards our whole lives. Our eyes move to her face, take it in, and say yes, that's Marilyn Monroe's face: I recognize the highly arched dark eyebrows, the short platinum mess of curls falling on her forehead just so, I know the straight-ahead look, open and startled and wistful, the lushly painted red lips, slightly parted, slightly panting, as if caught in the act of something, the small dark dot of a beauty mark strategically tattooed in the middle ground between the tip of her nose and the curve of her mouth. The image clicks so perfectly into what we know. There's nothing unfamiliar about her face to stop us from moving on to the next image to look at, the next thing to read, the next thing to consume.

After all these years of looking at her, what would be required to make us see Marilyn Monroe in a new way? Would she have to be cut up into little fragments and rearranged? Would she have to be propped before us exposed, stripped of makeup and clothes after twenty sleepless nights and standing in the snow, or buried in a mound of dirt like a sad clown, with a fig leaf in her teeth and top hat perched on her beautiful head?

Up until Milton Greene's portraits of Marilyn in fifty-two themed sittings, like a portfolio of essays, each with a slightly different persona, a different made-up self, photographs of Marilyn were either taken on sets or were glamour shots. With Greene, Marilyn participated in creating the poses—gypsy, saloon girl, circus performer, barely clad ballerina. My photo is one of the best known from the Ballerina Sitting, and is sometimes called *Marilyn Monroe in Tutu.* The sitting took place at Greene's studio in New York City in 1954. Ann Klein sent the ballerina dress to the studio, but it was two sizes too small. Most of the poses from the sitting are the result of Marilyn holding the dress together.

I'm looking at the way her dress opens up, the word would be *gapes,* when I notice the spots sprinkled liberally over her chest up to her neck. Are they freckles? Some of them are big, and might be small moles. I never noticed moles on Marilyn Monroe's chest before. Either they've been carefully camouflaged in her glamour photographs or I didn't look carefully. She has slightly splotchy skin. But here's the thing: I find the freckled, mottled skin endearing—more than endearing, I find it compelling, so much more interesting than the alabaster body achieved through thick layers of pancake makeup or airbrushing away all signs of life. There is nothing duller than a smooth, perfect-skinned woman. Marilyn has a trail of freckles leading down to her nipples. We can't see how far they go, but we can speculate, we can guess, and I guess they go pretty far. Her skin looks like real flesh that has burned in the sun, that flushes red during sex and takes a long time to calm down and compose itself. The skin tone of her chest is defiantly not the tone of her face, which has been made metaphorical by heavy makeup.

Her roughened skin leads me to her arms—the left one is bent awkwardly behind her and disappears into the tissue of her costume, a romantic tutu made of net and soft pink tulle. She's gripping the dress to keep it from slipping further. She rests her right arm on her leg and bends it up from the elbow so that her outstretched hand reaches her collarbone and her index finger points up to her face as if she were caught mid-sentence. She might be saying something profound, quoting Tolstoy—"It is amazing how complete is the delusion that beauty is goodness." Or something mundane like "God, what I'd give for a cup of coffee."

So much vies for attention. There's tension in the portrait—between the sculptural perfection of her face and the fleshiness of her body, between the hand pointing up to her manicured lips and the vulnerability of her feet, between the childlike tutu and the adult sexuality it can't control. Real ballerinas look otherworldly in their dresses, slender, mobile dolls whose sliver of humanness has been eradicated in their complete inhabitation of their role. Marilyn pours out of her costume; the ballerina dress, like so many other dresses she wore, will not contain her. She is not a doll, not a ballerina. She is a woman who is more comfortable in a state of undress. There's a curious incandescence under her skin that bubbles up and spills over.

In looking at Marilyn, I can't keep myself out of the picture. I remember a dress I wore in college that bears a resemblance to Marilyn's ballerina dress. I had been cast in the role of Heavenly Finlay in *The Sweet Bird of Youth*, which calls for Heavenly to "parade" about in a white dress as the perfect virgin. The limited resources of the college had turned up exactly one dress properly virginal for me to wear—a strapless white chiffon whose bodice was form fitting and whose skirt sashayed. The problem was it didn't fit. Like Marilyn's, it was two sizes too small. In other photos from the Ballerina Sitting, you see that the back of her dress was unfastened, held together by her hand or simply left drifting open to expose the slope of her back. It wasn't an option for me to hold the dress loosely upon my body, allowing it to slip and slide. I was pushed and prodded into the dress—many hands did the work, and I was told to hold my breath until the tracks of the zipper could be closed. It was a coffin of a dress.

In a photographic still from the production I am seated in my white dress upon a chair in the center of the stage's black space just like Marilyn. Only Marilyn manages to look at ease in a dress that won't stay put, and I look like I am embarrassed. I can't lean forward or move or smile. I can't breathe and my breasts are going to pop right out of that dress. Playing Heavenly may have been my greatest performance. I was anything but a reed-like virgin; I may have been the only married student at Pomona College. I couldn't think about my lines or who I was supposed to be because all my energy was focused on staying inside the dress, terrified that if I exhaled or moved suddenly, the zipper, so laboriously cleaving together, would undo itself and the whole length of the dress would heave apart, and I, in my fleshiness would fall out for the world to see, or at least those in the audience.

I had a body more like Marilyn Monroe's than Twiggy's, but unlike Marilyn, I didn't know what to do with mine. I wanted to put my body into a big sack and throw it to the back of the closet with all the rest of my messy life. I spent my youth trying to fit that dress, fastening zippers, buttoning buttons, cramming myself into a smaller size made for a different body. Marilyn was happiest when her clothes were falling off; the halls in her house were littered with discarded dresses, underwear, and, of course, shoes.

"Do you have a thing for feet, a foot fetish?" the clerk asks with more than a hint of aggression.

"Not that I know of," I reply, looking sheepishly down at my feet sheathed in worn-out boots, standing solidly on the linoleum floor made filthy by holiday shoppers. Shopping carts clog the aisles, pushed by bundled-up women looking for bargains on ornaments and artificial wreaths. When I stop to listen, I hear the endless clattering of wheels.

But maybe I do notice feet more than the average person. When I think of my mother, I think of her feet. Their extreme narrowness meant that she was forever twisting them; they just gave out without warning. Her feet were like willow-thin canoes: size nine, quadruple A. That's 9AAAA. Better as the subject of photography than as the proper foundation to support her. I inherited my mother's flat skinny feet and passed them onto my daughter: we are the women of useless feet. Pretty to look at, but they break down when we try to cross the street. Dancing in a tight dress across a treacherous stage in high heels is out of the question. Given this personal history, I look to see whether a person stands on sturdy feet or doesn't. I ask: how wide is her stance, how high is her arch, does she totter on tiny feet in bondage to her past?

Marilyn Monroe stood on sturdy feet. Her feet were perfectly proportionate to the rest of her body. A very average size seven. Not too thin, not too wide, just right, with a good arch to support her. She did not totter in high heels. But in the photos that weren't movie stills or publicity shots, she is often shoeless, running on the beach, lying on beds, chaises longues, beach blankets, talking on the phone at home, or famously reading James Joyce's *Ulysses* on a jungle gym, scrunching up her toes. The woman liked to go barefoot. She liked to touch the ground, feel where she was even when reading. In her "jump" portrait taken by Phillippe Halsman in 1954, she achieves the height and compactness of a trained gymnast. She hangs in black space, in nothingness, yet it's as if an invisible thread, an electrical connection of some sort, runs from her head to the ground, powering her and mooring her to the spot, drilling a hole where she'll eventually land.

Some people cover lots of miles in their lives, traveling a far distance from where they began. Marilyn Monroe's nomadic life began as an orphan, and she was in and out of different residences her whole life, never staying long anywhere. The number of her addresses exceeds the number of years she lived. She once said she never belonged to anything or anyone. Her life a series of arrivals and departures, hellos and goodbyes.

And some people dwell, circling where they are in ever penetrating waves that make their way down.

She wanted to get somewhere—fame, success, stardom. And early on she was willing to do what it took to reach her goals. But part of her was a dweller, someone who wanted to kick off her high-heel shoes so her feet could touch the ground, to bury her toes in sand, someone who wanted to get down and dirty, down real deep, and who wanted to stay in one place, where she could turn from east to west, and north to south, to see where in the world she belonged. After the end of her marriage to Arthur Miller, she bought the first residence that would be hers alone in Brentwood, California. She had this latin inscription embedded in the tiles at the entrance: "Cursum Perficio," or "I have completed my journey."

Greene hasn't subjected Marilyn to any radical reinvention or artistic assault. Yet his portrait has made me see something new about one of the most photographed women in the world. Perhaps finding something new involves more than just the composition of the photograph. Perhaps it involves more than just looking carefully. I had to enter the photo, get inside it, move up and down and up again, from side to side, circling the photo from all angles and yet holding all its parts in my head.

I've chosen my wood and glass, paid my bill, and take a last look at Marilyn before handing her over for framing. To the clerk and the people waiting in line behind me, I say, *Your eye wants to go elsewhere. But do not cast it on the varicolored portraits lined up by Warhol, the drooping, heavy eyes, the damaged lines of dialogue and empty set, the bottles of Nembutal. Look at her feet, will you. Look at her amazingly alive feet.*

SIDESTROKE

My Mother's Toenails

As her memory darkened, I did not see my mother. What hold time held upon my mother loosened and, like a shawl, slipped. My father worried that she would walk out the front door in her nightgown, with an empty black purse slung over her arm, into traffic she would not see, having forgotten her glasses on the nightstand. She might spread her high pink-paneled arms, with head sunk low, stretching both arms together until she was out of view.

She slept soundly, great pink flamingo arms fanning across the pillows into the bright morning. She saw no reason to get up. One day became the next, a piece in a featureless run of time. Late she rose on thin, ungainly legs, calling out for my father in a voice unsteady, and then made her way into the living room, where he had been reading for hours. By noon she grew soft and weepy and collapsed on the couch for her afternoon nap. Often she seemed to be walking with a man she thought was her father, side by side through an apple orchard in a place she once lived.

I should not have allowed my father to cancel my visits because of my mother's mood swings. Fearing she might completely disappear, I showed up on their doorstep without warning. I arrived on a scalding August morning and parked among the smoldering Buicks and Mercurys in the parking lot adjacent to the complex of condominiums where they had moved. My father puffed toward me on the narrow pathway and then guided me through their quarters. Two bedrooms, one for my mother, one for my father, anchored opposite ends of the condominium. Both doors were closed. In response to my father's call, out of one of these bedrooms emerged my mother in a long flamingo nightgown.

The woman who shuffled into the room, who had spent eighty years maintaining an impeccable, dignified appearance, no longer made the effort. Everything had fallen—her features, her shoulders, her chest, the last of her arches. Her glasses, bent and dirty, slid down her bruised and mottled nose. She was a shy child who had been coaxed from behind the closet door where she had been hiding. She seemed apologetic, yet I thought I caught a glint of mischievousness, as if her appearance were a disguise she had assumed to shock me. My father, practiced in covering her lapses, said, "Look, Marjorie—Marcia is here to see you." Five minutes later, she may not have known me. Abrasions and scabs ran up and down her arms and legs, which she scratched as in a daze. She laughed at something and then suddenly began to weep. I moved down the couch to be closer to her. She turned to me and said, "Baby girl, my lost girl."

Her feet were housed in white, open-toed satin slippers. Her nails had grown so long that they curled over her toes and underneath, spreading upon the floor. They were a thick, waxy yellow, hard and prehistoric. Did she not notice? She had to notice, for she couldn't walk properly, scuttling across the floor like a crab. Perhaps the nails had grown so tough, so thick and obdurate, that she no longer had the strength to cut them. My sister had spoken to me about my mother's toenails, how ashamed my father was of her that he wouldn't take her out, and yet how hesitant my sister was to cross one of the final boundaries into matters of personal hygiene. She had located a podiatrist who made house calls but was booked until mid-September. No one knew whether my mother would allow a stranger to attend to her feet.

At first I had to avert my eyes from my mother's toenails. It unsettled me to see how she had been robbed of her humanity. But I was wrong. After a while, her toenails no longer bothered me. I found an emotional core of many colors that, radiating outward, gave her a new kind of loveliness—not the beauty of physical care and perfection, but something more essential, perhaps seen only when the body has been harvested.

Two days before the appointment with the podiatrist, my mother suffered a massive cerebral hemorrhage. She went to her death with her toenails unclipped, intact.

The Reading

Before leaving for the reading, you washed your face and hands. Washing your face and hands, whether dirty or not, is something you do before and after events requiring reserves of resilience. You stopped mid-lather and looked up to see yourself in the Sheraton's mirror shortly before 3:00 p.m. Reaching for the towel, you asked yourself what you saw when you looked in the mirror. You decided that at this moment in the overheated Sheraton bathroom, you should avert your eyes. You could hear the creaks and cracks as you moved about the furniture of your face.

You exited the room and then the hotel through the back doors that opened onto the pedestrian plaza where an overweight woman seated by the fountain was singing Irish ballads in a mournfully high soprano voice. Two signs were taped to the front of her chair, which may or may not have been a wheelchair. You didn't know for sure because you swept by in a hurry. No one stopped to listen, and no one placed money in the soprano's donation box. All along the pedestrian way you heard the woman's high unfettered voice singing.

The reading was held in a ballroom. When you arrived, the fourteen readers had begun to seat themselves in the first two rows on the right side of the room. A few nonreaders were sprinkled among the group like spies. The podium careened to the right, off center on the stage, and everyone in attendance had shifted toward it in a sliding, lopsided motion like a broken plow. You took a seat on the aisle in the second row. You glanced about and saw that some of the readers were gloomy, even a little forlorn. One kept pushing his glasses up his nose though they had not slid down. In another, the jaw muscles flexed and quivered like a slide show depicting hard times. Often you thought you were the only writer who suffered at readings, but you saw now that you were wrong.

The writers were to read in alphabetical order, just like grade school and a whole lot of other martyr-making events where because of your last name you had to go first. Always first in school to present your report on Harriet Beecher Stowe or bread mold, you mumbled below hearing. Not first because of importance or merit, but first to break the trail, give the report, take the test, hit the ball, offer yourself up to the tribunal. If only you had a name later in the alphabet. You didn't want a name like Stoppit or Testerone; they came too late and besides belonged in the pages of the grotesque, but you'd be happy to have a name ending in the letter H. Let the ABCDEFG's exert themselves to warm up the crowd, and then turn it over to the H's for a while. But no, you were an early alphabet, a figure who for the daring required of you should be equipped with flying cape and steed. Alas no such flare and vertical capacity sprang from your spine.

When you mounted the stage, you didn't say that it was a miracle you had a copy of your piece, "My Mother's Toenails," which would be forthcoming soon in print. You didn't tell the audience that the printout of "My Mother's Toenails" was lying on your desk at home in a different Midwestern state right next to the forgotten list of things to remember for your trip. The list and the forgotten "Toenails" reminded you of that joke about the lazy man who sits down to watch TV without his remote and wishes he had a remote for his remote. You had never managed to put the printout into your bag. You didn't tell them that you had two classes, each two hours long, three appointments, and one meeting the day before you left. That you returned one set of memoirs and a quiz on the differences between the short story and personal essay and had given a sensitive response to the fifth installment of a ten-thousand-word consideration of a boating excursion on a small lake by an independent-study student named Grim. Or that between these duties you drove out to the airport to pick up a plane ticket for your daughter from a man whose stomach fell to his knees. You didn't tell them how he propped his stomach on the counter while he scheduled your daughter's flights with a kindness you were unaccustomed to. How you wondered if his stomach was the result of absorbing other people's sorrow. You often thought that people with great stomachs were absorbing the world's sorrow, the sorrow that seeps out of car windows and suitcases at the passenger drop-off. You didn't tell them how you woke up that morning at the Sheraton, looked through your papers, and did not find "My Mother's Toenails." How you ransacked your suitcase, sifted through the piles of conference material in vain.

That morning you had gone to the bookstore thinking perhaps the review in which "Toenails" was to be published had come in and you would be saved. It hadn't. You ran into two writers and told them about your dilemma. They challenged you to write a new essay; you had the time, they said, a few hours. You should be able to come up with 750 words by 3:00 p.m. Just recount what happened, they said: a writer forgets her material. Then you should explain why, they said—top it off with some sprinkles of reflection. What would Freud say? He was a reliable guide to composition on this subject. Freud would say the reader left her work at home to escape an occasion of judgment. The reader had not consciously decided to back out and save herself. She didn't *mean* to leave the piece at home. But Freud would say that the reader had preemptively shot herself in the foot to inflict the wounding she thought would be forthcoming from others. Freud would go on to explain whence in early life the damage got started. He might bring up the etymology of the name Oedipus, that is, "Swollen Foot." But you only had 750 words. Thanks for the help, you said as you turned away. The writers at the bookstore leaned against a pile of nonfiction mysteries and concluded you were like a lot of other smart screw-ups hoping for grace.

You didn't tell the audience that you walked back to the hotel having decided there was nothing to do but reconstruct the original "Toenails"—all 750 words. You sat at the desk outfitted with silver ice bucket, coffee maker, and an array of cups. You were not thirsty. Outside the wind was fierce and you imagined a long procession of people and the dusky sounds of swirling leaves. You began, *As her memory darkened, I did not see my mother.* You said each word out loud as you pressed it upon the page, scratching out words and then replacing them. More words came. *Her nails had grown so long that they curled over her toes and underneath, spreading upon the floor. They were a thick, waxy yellow, hard and prehistoric. Did she not notice? She had to notice, for she couldn't walk properly, scuttling across the floor like a crab. Perhaps the nails had grown so tough, so thick and obdurate, that she no longer had the strength to cut them.* The reconstruction of "Toenails" took two hours and your hand burned all the way up to the elbow. You were uncertain whether this version you had written out was identical to the one you left at home, but you were surprised how the sentences came back to you, floated up, thick and hard and intact as your mother's toenails. Perhaps there was another reason you left your piece at home besides the foot wound and all. Perhaps you needed to hear the words come back to you like this, discovering them all over again. The piece was a living thing inside you now, not a printout lying on your desk.

You said none of this to the audience that skidded over to the chairs on the right side. You carried your handwritten pages up to the podium and began as if nothing troubled you. *As her memory darkened, I did not see my mother. What hold time held upon her loosened and, like a shawl, slipped.* As you read, your mother appeared before you as she had in your final visit, freed of her torn life, you freed from your torn life with your mother, and your mother was beautiful. *I found an emotional core of many colors, that, radiating outward, gave her a new kind of loveliness—not the beauty of physical care and perfection, but something more essential, perhaps seen only when the body has been harvested.* And then you were finished and you dismounted the stage and returned to your seat on the aisle in the second row of chairs among the piecemeal hearers whose faces now were vivid as a Sappho fragment in the beautiful ballroom, and the next writer took the stage and the next after that, a long procession and all of them beautiful.

Then the reading was over. People who knew you said to you the things people who know you say.

Back through the pedestrian plaza you were the stranger, walking toward the woman singing. In the hours you had been away the singer's voice had lost its pitch and was splitting at the high notes. Still she kept singing with a secret strength that you felt in your own body. It was indeed a wheelchair. You took out your wallet and deposited a sum in the box before continuing to the hotel and the room and to the bathroom where you washed your hands and to the mirror, to which you returned your eyes and in which you dusted your face.

I, Swimmer

"Here's money for lunch," my mother said with a crisp click of her purse. I took the coins in my fist and, working to push open the broad door of the Buick, slid off the seat and down onto the grass that bordered the parking lot. There I stood in my red bathing suit between two old elms, shucked like an ear of corn, hesitating.

"That way," my mother said, dropping her head to point through the windshield at a bending gravel path beside the golf course. With the same hand and one motion, she shifted the transmission into park and slid over the seat to yank my door shut. The enormous station wagon wheeled around and lumbered away over the hot asphalt, spitting raspy gravel from its tires.

My mother was not a swimmer and did not enjoy the pool scene at the country club. She preferred bridge and crossword puzzles indoors, and was of an age to keep herself out of the scorching sun.

Still I stood within the quiet elms. A minute later another car arrived in the lot and parked. The rear doors opened in perfect synchrony and two girls popped out, and then from the driver's seat emerged a woman in bathing attire. The girls, issuing mutual challenges, raced away to the gravel path while the woman hurried behind in her flapping sandals, calling failed admonitions of restraint.

I followed her. The path cut through the deep green lawn, curved right around a stand of trees, and rose to a plateau, where the clubhouse came into view. When I reached the top, I saw that on the other side of the hill the path dipped down to a flat basin, longer and wider than a football field. And there within it were the glittering pools, a square, a rectangle, and a bean, set like sapphires in a tiara with a yoke of profoundest green. My heart lifted, and I stepped quickly down the path toward the churning crowd of people below.

What a riot of color and activity! Fiesta-colored towels and beach baskets were strewn across lounge chairs behind busy mothers and children who swarmed in and about the waters, toddlers splashing in the shallow baby pool, mothers glistening in suntan oil as they perched on the rim, each keeping an eye on her young. The lap pool, the longest and grandest, was set in the middle. At one end, graduates from the baby pool were learning to jump off the edge into mothers' arms. In the near corner, girls were practicing water acrobatics, turning somersaults and pointing their legs into the air like steeples. At the black one-third line, older women in bathing caps with elaborate flowers blooming near their ears swam on their sides, heads out of water to keep their lipstick dry, crossing the width like slow drifting spars. Teenagers tried to swim laps, navigating around the small cities of commerce that blocked the lanes.

The third pool, the diving pool, cradled by a stand of weeping willows, was the most beautiful. With the greatest depth, its blue was austere, a marine blue.

I didn't know how to join in. I laid out my towel and eased into the lap pool between the leapers-into-arms and the acrobats, clasping the edge and recasting my eyes to the enormous sun light.

I was dropped off every day, and soon I was soaked up by the combustion of kids screaming "Marco Polo" or absorbing themselves in quieter games. I made friends with some of the children, and their mothers adopted me in their way, wrapping me in a towel when I stood shivering. Still I missed my mother—not so much my mother, as someone to be my guardian, to watch out for me, to worry, as the hours went by, that I was getting sunburned.

There were times when I was alone, when I had been dropped off before the others arrived or was picked up late by my father on his way home from work. In the early morning or evening, the waters were almost military in their bearing, geometric shapes serene in their own right. What I liked to do then was hold my breath underwater in the cold diving pool. I'd sit Buddha-style on the ledge cut into the side of the pool, submerged a few feet below the surface, where no one could easily see me, as if frozen within a cube of ice. I stayed under for as long as possible, still as an idol, until my lungs rebelled. Then I'd push off from the ledge and break the surface into the blue heavens above. This was my ritual, hundreds of incarnations on my infinite path to enlightenment.

"You should learn to swim," my father said one afternoon when he came to pick me up from the pools. Watching from the clubhouse veranda in his blue seersucker suit, he had seen me splash through the water in a motion of my own design, part doggy paddle, part frog, like a spawn of mis-speciation who could not find a stroke appropriate to her conformation. I was in my ninth year, and that summer I was sent to Mosey Wood, a Girl Scout camp that lay along a lake in the Poconos.

It was my first experience of swimming outside a pool's tight frame. An instructor in water safety taught me how to extend my frog paddle into the breaststroke, to link all my movements in one fluid, continuous motion, so that I was close to being human in the water. I discovered I had a gift for swimming long distances, born from an ability to withstand cold temperatures. Unlike the other young campers, I wasn't afraid of being alone in the deepest part of the lake, where my sometimes-burdensome solitude became an asset. By the end of the summer I had become the youngest ever to earn the coveted purple cap for swimming the lake's length. Campers and counselors from my unit met me with cheers when I reached the other side.

Proud of this accomplishment, my father signed me up for the club's swimming team. A deeply competitive man, he told me stories about his youthful feats in watersport. His preferred event was the crawl, the most propulsive of strokes. He wished his only child to follow in his footsteps and interpreted my success at long distances as evidence of a competitive spark. But in meets I was rarely the best—I came in second or third or farther back among the also-rans. I swam competitively for many years without turning into a top-ranked swimmer. What I loved about swimming was that only then was I peacefully alone.

The summer before my sophomore year in high school, I returned to a lake, this time with a boy. Billy was three years my senior and had a summer job at our club, teaching tennis to the young. I was apprentice to his tutoring, and I conducted my flirtation on court, hitting with a lot of speed. He was graceful, getting to the ball easily, his strokes effortless and fluid. But I was a fish out of water on the clay, sliding about and kicking up red flecks that always stained my whites.

Late in August Billy invited me to join his family for a weekend at their vacation home on Lake Naomi. I cannot now explain why he did it, but it was my sincere belief then that obscure currents flowing between us would lead to a momentous outcome, just as an oath on a tennis court led to the French Revolution, and that Billy's summer house was my Bastille. My feelings were better developed than his, I knew, but a pair of orchids doesn't bloom in unison. Given the chance, I might quicken him.

At Lake Naomi the houses were tucked far back from the road, with long gravel driveways through the woods. The emphasis was on privacy and acreage. Billy's house was made of Pennsylvania flagstone, with a massive stone fireplace, wood floors, and plenty of guest rooms.

The first night he introduced me to his friends, including a girl improbably named Wellesley. She was tall, dark-eyed, dark-skinned, dark-haired, substantial, self-assured, capable, with a soft laugh and comforting manner. I was thin and angular, jittery, a waif. I had light hair and thin feet—everything about me was light. In fact, Billy had been after me about my lack of weight, as if I lacked enough heft to be taken seriously. Right then Billy and Wellesley were at the broken-up stage of something on-again, off-again, but clearly that wasn't going to stick. By late Saturday, watching him seek her eyes amid the darkness of every room, I knew my chances were slipping away. Sunday found me desperate. I thought swimming the lake might make him love me.

I broached the subject, and for a lark the group went along to observe my feat. They giggled and straggled down to the lakeshore, while I waited nervously in my red suit in the shallow water. Billy took a seat in a canoe to follow me, and at the last minute, Wellesley joined him.

The water was marbled currents of warm and cold, and at first I made good progress across the lake. By the time I reached the deeper midpoint, however, I had used up my adrenaline, and the water turned frigid. It occurred to me that I might fail to reach the other side. I was sure Billy was bored or had forgotten me. Yet I was yoked to the canoe, as if I were pulling it across the lake.

I flailed to reach the far shore, staggering out of the water on shaking legs as I tried to gain land. Billy pulled the canoe up into the shore grass and wrapped me in towels, but not in his arms. His girl stood by his side with a look of concern. He marveled at my stamina and pitied me.

After that summer, swimming faded, like a novel that once meant everything to me but now gathered dust. The waters dried up, as it were. I swam from time to time but risked nothing and harvested no memories. Yet if someone were to ask, I would have said, "I am a swimmer."

Last fall I had a one-month residency at an artists' colony in Virginia. I dreamed about the leave, imagining that on this island of time I might take stock of whom I had become and whom I had lost. So much had come to pass: career, marriage, children born and grown, my mother dead, my father now a shambler in old age. There was a place to swim at the colony, I learned, and in anticipation I bought my first swimming suit in years. In the last days of September, I drove south to Virginia and took up my temporary abode in a converted barn. The first morning, I joined a group of three at breakfast who were discussing the nearby lake.

"It has a certain legendary status around here," said Judith, a veteran colonist and, I learned later, a painter. She suggested a swim that afternoon. "Visitors are often defined by whether they brave the lake," she said.

"I've just had eye surgery," said Allen, the eldest among us, "so I'm afraid I'll have to wade, not brave."

I tried to look nonchalant but noted the competitive edge in Judith's voice. "What is the difficulty with this lake?" I asked.

"There is the cold thrill of the turbid waters," she said in a manner both grand and sly, "and at one end there are beavers, snapping turtles, and snakes." Her eyes were bright, and on the right side her mouth turned awry. I noticed I was not alone in lacking enthusiasm. Imagine the scene: the lake circled by aspens and willows, heavy in dipping green. Myself slipping into the lake and swimming away from the shore, flanked on either side by waving blacksnakes. The image knotted me up instantly.

"I'll try the end *opposite* the wildlife," said Diana, the fourth at the table.

I doubted I had much left of my capacity to withstand cold, and the snakes repelled me. Perhaps, I thought, I have turned into someone who likes to keep dry. But if the lake meant self-definition, better to be game. When the appointed time for the swim came around that afternoon, I emerged from the barn in my bathing suit to meet the others for the short drive to the lake.

We parked at the end of the dirt road that descended from the paved highway. The lake, fronted by a boathouse and a substantial dock, was kidney-shaped and squirming under a brisk wind. Trees overhung the water thickly on all sides, dappled by the sun. It was a pretty spot, but I couldn't see beneath the soupy surface.

"Swimmers! Swimmers all!" shouted Diana as she loped down the dock.

"We go to the dam and back," Judith said to me. "It's about a mile."

We eased ourselves down the ladder at the end of the dock and shoved off—Diana in her large goggles and snorkel, Judith long and lean and fast away. Allen kept near our starting point.

It was stingingly cold. I swam with my head out of the water, my neck clenched, just lifting slightly to breathe. I followed the tack the other women took toward the dam, trying to stay roughly in the middle of the lake, as if veering to either side would bring me unknown harm. I slapped the water in a chop that my Mosey Wood instructors would never have forgiven, stroke after stroke, rushing forward as fast as I could. Without my glasses, the trees were a blur of greens and reds and yellows like a watercolor held too close. I would have liked to see where I was, how far from the boathouse, dam, and other swimmers. But this was not to be known. There could have been hikers circling the lake, deer in the woods on shore, blue herons stalking the far end. Dragonflies landed close by; I'd catch a glint of light, a slide of illuminated wing, and swim on.

I soon overtook Diana, reached the dam, and turned back. I never caught Judith, who waited for me back at the dock. Hauling myself up the ladder and into the sun, relieved that it was over, I was shamed by my shaking legs. But Judith surprised me, saying that I had a good stroke, a thing of beauty, really.

"Look there!" she said. Beyond the dam, at the far end of the lake, a head rose up out of the water, belonging to a sort of creature we could not identify.

"I didn't want to tell you," Judith confessed, "but swimming was banned in August due to fecal matter from the beavers. There was a sign. But the problem cleared up, and the sign was removed." You'd have to be more confident in signs than I to be reassured by this sequence. When I got back to my barn and took off my bathing suit, I scrubbed away a coat of dirt, and that night a rash appeared.

After a week of using the rash as an excuse, I rejoined the swimmers, determined to retackle this defining lake. This time I proceeded differently. I sat on the dock for a long while, warming in the sun. When I felt at home, less a stranger, I eased down the ladder and sat on the lowest rung, motions taken quietly. I pushed off and began zigzagging toward the dam. I no longer worried where I was in relation to the others, how far I lagged behind. If anyone was watching, I didn't know about it.

For the remainder of my stay, at the end of each long day, I was grateful to peel off my shoes and socks, run down the dock until I came to the last plank, and dive in head-first. The cold water allowed me to forget, to let go of whatever I had held too tightly. By the time I left Virginia, the lakescape had been stripped to its essence. All its parts dissolved in water, flower and rock, wind and cloud, tree and shore, woman and forgotten girl.

When I returned home from Virginia, I resolved to swim regularly, and found an indoor pool, designed for laps, at a local health club. The lighting is kept low, in a soft, ageless cast of anonymity, and the muted sounds from outside the gleaming glass walls doze on the breathing water.

On my way to the pool I pass through the women's locker room, its walls and floor tiled in shining white, past shower stalls, a steam room, a cold plunge and adjacent whirlpool. There sit women and girls of all ages side by side, round and soft as the shoulders of ripe plums, or lithe and smooth as daisy stems. Sometimes I join them to let the jets of hot water loosen the clenched muscle stays of my back. I walk deliberately to the painfully cold plunge-pool, step in, and submerge myself. I stay under for as long as I can bear, and resurface in a gush of water, pushing my hair back from my eyes, glad to cast about me yet again.

Swimming in a pool is like a meditation, an act of faith. I like to swim at night when the pool is illuminated with underwater lights. When I stand before it, on the verge of entering, I feel a lump in my throat, a homesickness. I carry no purse, no identification. What I have done or have not done lies behind me, my accomplishments and my mistakes deposited in a locker. In my bathing cap pulled low over my hair and ears, my goggles covering my eyes, no one knows me. There is nothing and no one to lean on. Other swimmers are there, shafts of moving color, but I am alone. We never exchange greetings; we've come for the silence. Someone sits in the lifeguard chair, a blotch of red. I see a blurry body of water before me like a blank sheet of paper. The water is cold, always a shudder when I first descend the steps. I push away and begin my breaststroke, in the first laps trying to quiet my mind, musing on my father astride the clubhouse veranda, watching with an opaque gaze, on stopwatches and canoes and far shores. Then I am a ship in a limitless ocean, and I have lost my bearings. I concentrate on laps, lap on lap; swimming is the only word my body says. I throw the spool of myself out and reel it in, over and over. I no longer know I am swimming.

The swimmer I want to be does not require acclimation; trepidation is not in her vocabulary. She wants quick immersion. Stripped of jewelry, not even a thin wedding band, the swimmer makes you believe she is unharnessed from the world, owns no clothes, belongs to no house, and that a heavy purse, with its wallet and identification cards, would drag her down. The swimmer swims for herself and checks her baggage before she enters the water. The swimmer I want to be stands in the middle of a blank canvas, facing forward with hands firmly on hips. The bend in her elbows makes a white space like the V of Canada geese in skies of migration. When I see her, I think water. It must be nearby, not far from the path of vision, not even a stone's throw away, for her stance is one of readiness. The canvas is blank, no pool, no lake, no ocean, no body of water the mind can see, yet everything suggests it is always at hand, that she carries water with her wherever she goes, ready to plunge in. *Plunge in,* I say.

Sidestroke

With *side*, we see a woman in repose, lying on the left or right wall of her body, resting in bed like a dormant oar. With *stroke*, we see her hand's unbroken sweep across some surface, a cat, a man, a lake. Add *stroke* to *side* and she is no longer in stasis. She is living, moving, caressing, no matter how languid that movement might be.

The word can be split in two or kept united, *side stroke* or *sidestroke*, but regardless, the swimmer addresses the water laterally, not face down, not on her back.

Associations: the maternal. The recommended position for pregnant women at rest in bed is SOS, sleeping on side, because it promotes the flow of blood to the placenta.

What it is not: It is not a competitive stroke. No matter how finely you tune your technique, slicing the water with a scissoring kick, you will not be entering any races. The stroke holds little attraction for male athletes. *Note*: I've never encountered a man swimming on his side, nor can I picture a man doing the necessary stroke. A man would not be featured in a textbook illustration of this approach to propulsion.

If someone told me a man had been seen swimming the sidestroke, I would ask for verification. (But see addendum below.)

Use (1): Rescue maneuvers. Recall lifesavers with one arm locked around a body on its back, limp, waterlogged, the one arm a hook that clamps drowner to swimmer, whose form is rotated to its side, a flotation device, her head up, her other arm free, lifting and pulling like the boom of a crane, laboriously rafting toward a far shore. That is the sidestroke.

Aside: My grandmother saved a person from drowning using just such a stroke. In the photo in the newspaper clipping, her arm forms a bold arc like a wishbone, curving across the man's chest. Dead before I was born, she was a mystery to me, by repute a dominating being, bending people to her will. As I hold the photo of my grandmother's heroic stroke, her arm reaches out of the frame to clasp me to her.

Use (2): It is often used for long-distance swimming that requires great stores of endurance. Energy is expended slowly and steadily and thus lasts a long time—something akin to the dispersing of energy in giving birth. *Addendum:* Navy SEALs learn a version of the stroke that uses more scissor kicking, less arm movement. Candidates for naval special warfare must be able to swim four miles in ocean water, with advanced gear, using the CSS, the combat sidestroke.

The sidestroke thus is sometimes swum by one whose purpose is to traverse great spaces in stealth while complex secrets burden her.

Viewpoint: Some commentators see it as a remnant of an earlier stage of swimming, an anomaly, an archaic remain of strokes long surpassed on the evolutionary chain. Like women riding horses sidesaddle. *Question:* Were the sidestroke and sidesaddle invented to handicap women, to disqualify them from taking jumps or waves head on? Or was modesty invented to handicap women, and the sidesaddle and sidestroke followed as the means?

Focus: The sidestroke offers a one-sided perspective on the body of water. One does not look up at the sky or down to the depths. It is hard to see where one is going. One is in the middle of things.

Personal History: When my mother swam, she was unique, for her only technique was the sidestroke. When I watched her swim, I thought *unusual, quaint, singular.* As a young girl I was embarrassed by the spectacle she made as she rose from her lounge chair, clad in a one-piece suit of bold floral design, tightened on with a zipper. Her bathing cap, secured with a chin strap, rhymed with the suit, in the colors of exotic flowers—fuchsia, tangerine, peach, hyacinth blue. Over one ear, pasted onto the fabric, a flower bloomed, open to the size of a ruffled peony. It was always this side she held aloft as she glided through the water, a prom corsage drifting down a long, sustaining dream.

See: Esther Williams, competitive swimmer turned movie actress, and popular from the mid-1940s into the 1950s. She must have influenced my mother. *Bathing Beauty*, released in 1944, was the first of her aqua-musicals, and elaborations like *Neptune's Daughter* and *Million Dollar Mermaid* came out in 1952. Esther wore a classic sheath, an all-in-one bathing suit, with stiff bra cups and boning, complete with zippers. She had firm, long legs, perfect posture, and a high-wattage smile, a description that fit my mother as well. Her adaptation of the Williams mode was watered down a bit; after all, she was swimming at the Lehigh Valley Country Club, not on a Hollywood movie set. Still, my mother's style, which made something cinematic of herself, was a little outlandish in the middle of a cornfield. One could admire her audacity. She gave serious consideration to the question of how a woman should be groomed to swim, how to make a splash, but ignored the matter of prowess. The synchronized swimming that Esther Williams spawned depends upon an aesthetics of costume and athletic tautness. My mother ignored the athletics.

Paradox: I was a competitive swimmer from an early age, and above all else desired to be a force in the water. I wanted to swim like my grandmother, not my mother.

Now at the pool my purposes are more dispersed. I wear a silicone cap that hugs my skull, without chin strap or flower, and my suit is a Speedo. My face is scrubbed clean and goggles protect my eyes, because I immerse my head. For three-quarters of my session, I swim with vigor. My strokes are powerful, fast, and cut through the water. I have a rotation—crawl, breast, back. I'm flutter-kicking up a storm.

Then, as I flip at the wall, I morph into a full-blown rose. Something comes over me and I'm on my side, moving slowly up the lane. Inexplicably, under no threat of coercion, of my own free will, I swim the much-reviled stroke. I am the only performer of the sidestroke at the pool where I swim.

Story: Now I can tell a story. The title of the story is "Sentence."

"Sentence": When I swim the sidestroke, I become my mother.

Denouement: The punch or surprise doesn't come first. This is a complex sentence, a tangled sentence: the subordinate clause needs the main clause to complete it: *When I swim the sidestroke* depends upon *I become my mother*. When I am alone swimming the sidestroke, I have no purpose, I am incomplete. What if I shake things up, resist this conclusion, swim upstream? *I become my mother when I swim the sidestroke*. Even when the subordinate clause comes first, the main clause dominates the emotional hierarchy. Grammar mirrors psychology.

Diagram:

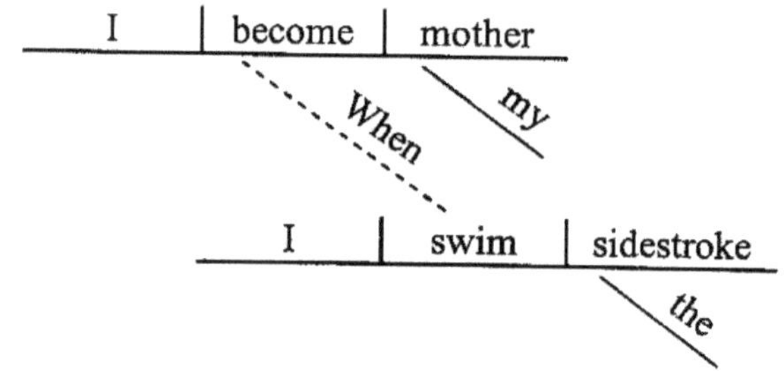

Who is speaking?

Interpretation (1): An epic treatise on failure packed into a teacup, the blink of an eye. A tragedy.

In "Sentence," the fusion of identities is not a happy resolution of the rising action. The daughter's becoming her mother, perhaps aging into the mother, is not the happy fate she was seeking. The daughter would have done just about anything not to become her mother. She agitated her whole life to establish a separate identity untainted by her mother's rule and character, by languid movements and style. Her finding herself, in the end, regardless of epic struggle, swimming the sidestroke signals a collapse of tragic proportions. She knows her failure. The daughter has mastered all the strokes, assiduously avoiding only the one, which yet overtakes her, a force larger than herself, a force she doesn't understand and can't untangle, like a sentence decreed and imposed, a narrative of captivity.

Interpretation (2): A comedy.

All's well that ends well. 1. The mother is resurrected in the daughter. 2. The daughter is emancipated by becoming her mother. 3. The daughter makes peace with the mother she was born to. 4. One can no longer separate daughter from mother, mother from daughter. They have metamorphosed into one. 5. Generations are reconciled in the figure of the swimmer and the motion of the sidestroke. 6. We're all the same deep down, floating down a dream stream on our sides. 7. Laugh, the sentence seems to be saying. Mother's got the last laugh.

Autumn Sonata

I wonder if anyone understands Ingmar Bergman's 1978 film meditation on the knotted relations of mothers and daughters, *Autumn Sonata*, as well as I do. Surely, I am not so peculiar, so singular, I hope, in recognizing in the portrait some of my own experiences with my mother, how we wanted things from each other that neither of us could give. There must be multitudes of mothers and daughters, of daughters become mothers, who see themselves in the characters Ingrid Bergman and Liv Ullman play and ask whether they will ever stop being mother and daughter. Watching the film by myself thirty years after its release, I feel I could have written its script. Some of the dialogue is so close to lines I've written as to feel indistinguishable from my own.

My husband watched the movie at his friend's house one Sunday night when I couldn't join them. Upon returning home, he insisted I watch the movie before he mailed it back to Netflix. Initially I thought his urgency in having me watch was based on the excellence of the movie, and he did speak of its marvels, particularly the early key scene when after dinner Eva plays the Chopin Prelude No. 2 in A Minor for her mother and husband. The camera rests on the face of her mother, a famous concert pianist, for the duration of her daughter playing the prelude. The look on Charlotte's face is more than disappointment that her daughter plays so poorly and with such undisciplined emotion. She looks pained. While the mother doesn't directly condemn her daughter's rendition, she does something much worse: she undermines her daughter's confidence, making her doubt whether she grasps the emotional tenor of the music, and destroys her pleasure in playing the piano. She manages to manipulate Eva into insisting that her mother play the piece to show her how it should be done. Her mother, who has spent a lifetime performing Chopin, performs a version that far surpasses Eva's amateurish version. We, who are watching, are meant to feel this is a familiar pattern between the two: the mother trumps the daughter. We see in Eva's expression a lifetime of never pleasing her mother and it's devastating.

My husband was primarily interested in Bergman's mastery in conveying so much about the characters and their history through their relationships to the Chopin piece, and he noted that both Eva and her mother played the entire piece in the movie. He thought this an extraordinary risk for Bergman to take—wouldn't there be a chance that viewers would be bored to hear the same piece of music twice, back to back? At first I focused on what interested my husband, agreeing that it was a notable accomplishment that Bergman made Charlotte's disposition on Chopin's Prelude No. 2 interesting in its own right and meaningful for the film. But I found my attention straying to the question of why the daughter, Eva, chose to play the piano when her mother was an extraordinary musician. Why didn't she choose some other instrument or other pursuit altogether? And if she must play the piano why did she volunteer to play Chopin? She was making a martyr of herself, knowingly offering herself up to her mother's withering gaze. Wouldn't she have learned to protect herself from such an inevitable and unflattering comparison? I was flooded with questions and I hadn't even seen the movie. My husband responded to my barrage by saying yes those are some of the questions underlying the daughter's behavior. And then he gave me a knowing look. I began to fear that he believed this movie would have special significance to me, as someone who had suffered at the hands of her mother. Did I want to watch the movie? Did I need to confront yet again that the need for a mother's approval and love never ends and the remarkable lengths daughters will go to achieve that illusive happy end?

I was curious, of course. It had been a long time since I watched a Bergman film. I remembered most of his films as black and white and bleak, alternating between lots of talking and utter silence. They weren't films to forget. Eventually I determined to watch the film and settled into bed alone several nights later and began. It's a relatively short, economical movie, about ninety minutes, and yet even so, I couldn't watch to the end. And somewhere before I stopped the DVD, I found that I couldn't make myself look at the screen. I was looking away as if I was watching the slaughter of animals. After I stopped the DVD and language about starting again appeared, I wondered if I'd return and finish it. Everything in the movie was hitting too close to home for an impartial, distant viewing. Even now I can't begin to evaluate the film.

For starters, Ingrid Bergman, at the age of sixty-two, resembled my mother. They might have been twins except for the accent. Tall and imposing, they had a regal physical presence—standing very straight. In the opening scene when Charlotte arrives at her daughter's house for a visit, she's wearing a camel colored pants suit, just like the suits my mother favored. Camel colored—her color. Tasteful, Smart, Becoming. Ingrid Bergman wore her hair cut short, not too short, but chin length, dyed brown with some gray showing through at the temples, and her hair was curled away from her face just like my mother's. In one scene, midway through, she's woken up from a bad dream and comes into the living room where her daughter is sitting. It's the middle of the night. She's wearing no makeup and she's in the grip of an unhappy combination of emotions—fear, self-pity, yearning. She begins what I'd call a monologue, although her daughter is in the room, about how her parents neglected her when she was a child, how they never touched her, how she knew nothing of warmth or intimacy. She's feeling sorry for herself, in full daughter mode, without any recognition of the damage her lack of warmth as a mother has caused her own daughter, how she has passed on a legacy of distance. She could have been my mother—my mother said these same things about her early life and in the same tone and with the same facial expression, with a look of sadness that even as a child made me want to protect my mother. Eva sits and listens for a long time and then her pent-up hurt and anger begin to emerge, and she says things to her mother that make her cry. Instead of the mother mothering her daughter, the mother wants her daughter to mother her. How rich, I thought, after the earlier struggle over Chopin. Bergman gives us the mother in close-up and holds the camera on her face. The long minutes on her face nearly killed me. Her eyes, hazel-gray and lonely, were my mother's eyes, eyes weakened over time, eyes clouded with a combination of rage and fear. Charlotte's face, with her high cheekbones, broad forehead, strong mouth with full lips and perfect teeth: it was like looking at my mother.

Bergman's idea to show the mother watching her daughter play and then the daughter watching her mother play is one of the most brilliant and excruciating representations of the trouble between mothers and daughters. We watch the different kinds of pain percolate up from the inside to rearrange the furniture of their faces and neither of them can let what falls between them go. Charlotte must correct her daughter even at this late stage in their lives. This is a portrait of the mother as having no pity or empathy for her daughter, mother as competitive still, and selfish. And this is a portrait of the daughter who must subject herself once again to her mother's judgment, hoping against all experience that this time her mother will believe her daughter's happiness is worth more than her own. And when Charlotte chooses herself, again, as we know she will, Eva can't bear it.

Usually we think the natural order is for the daughter to overwrite or supersede the mother as sons take over their fathers' businesses, but not so here. It is the mother who must have the last word, who must outperform her daughter even though there is no audience in attendance to cheer. And yet, for me at least, Charlotte's performance is not definitive and does not entirely erase Eva's. Like a ghost print, the daughter's stumbling notes bleed through the mother's versions and ring in my ears.

A few days after I had stopped the movie, I returned to see it through. I've never been good at abandoning a book at the midpoint or walking out of a movie before the credits. No matter how difficult the viewing experience may prove, I have to see it through to the end. When *Autumn Sonata* was over, when mother and daughter had said their goodbyes in a moment of fragile resolution that I knew wouldn't last, I decided to clean.

I chose the living room, the most heavily trafficked room in the house, where registers blow the dirt up from the floor to settle on every surface like a layer of river sediment. I began with the mantle outfitted with photos of my children and moved in a circle throughout the room, ending with the sideboard, always reserved for last because of its difficulty. What is the difficulty with this sideboard, you might ask. Well, for starters it's laden with bowls of shells my mother collected from the beach in Florida where she spent the last years of her life. Each fragile shell's ruffled flutes become coated in thick dust. Painstaking business, this dusting of the shells. Most of the time, I just move dust from one spot to another and think of my mother's brow brain and breast turned to soot in an urn the size of a telephone book. She cleaned the same glass balls, lifted each from the bowl where they were displayed, and polished with a soft cloth one might use for silver, placing each carefully back in its spot. She was meticulous about all. The house was never dirty—not even water spots on the bathroom counters or smudges on the mirrors. Beds were made with hospital corners. The horse figurines were well dusted on my bookshelf. My little desk stationed in front of the window was bare and the wood highly polished. If someone were to wander to my room and open the door, she would not think a little girl lived there. She would think my mother was childless.

My mother would be disappointed in my housekeeping as she was disappointed with most facets of my life. Animals have the run of the house, sleep in beds and couches at their pleasure. My children's rooms often post signs on the door saying disaster area or under construction, enter at your own risk. And the kitchen, well, let's just say you should be careful not to lean against the appliances. I tend to clean when I am low—there's nothing like sorrow or regret to spur getting out the dusting cloths. I hadn't planned to clean; it wasn't on my list. But after *Autumn Sonata* I found myself picking up the photograph of my mother in its tarnished sterling frame. The tarnishing begins the minute I put it back in its spot on the sideboard after polishing. And I can never remove the smudges my fingers make holding it. Even from across the room I can see the telltale signs.

I carried the photograph into the kitchen, where I keep the silver polish under the sink. I could barely see the silver for all the tarnish, though I polished it before my father's Christmas visit. I was thinking that it hadn't been that long ago and I don't know what else I was thinking, my usual chain of thoughts, I suppose, about how beautiful my mother was all through her life but especially in this photograph when she was a young college student full of dark beauty and emotional intensity, how there has never been and never will be anyone so influential in my life as my mother. She's been so gigantic that I spent most of my youth trying to get away from her. To no avail, of course, for she carved out a place so deep inside me that even if I went a long way away, she was still with me. I've carried my mother inside me and we have traveled a far distance from where we began. Even after her death it takes less than a second for her image to appear before me, for her voice saying my name to ring its sound. Whenever I look down at my hands, I see her hands lying over mine. All I write is covered with my mother's fingerprints.

I squeezed the tarnish remover onto the cloth and started to rub the frame's side, starting with the outer rims and making my way inside toward the photo itself, and the silver began to slowly emerge.

ENOUGH

Mothers, Writers

Harm

Do no harm. As a mother my job is to keep my children safe. To keep them from harm. Especially to not bring harm upon them myself. Can I do it? No chance. No one can protect their child absolutely. But that doesn't mean I don't try. I lie awake at night worrying, and when something harmful happens to my children, I feel I have failed. And there are all kinds of harms, so many possibilities.

Illnesses and genes that get passed along—some of what gets passed along isn't too terrible, like weak ankles or nearsightedness, but some can be serious, like diabetes or depression.

Accidents, falls, burns, crashes, pushes, shoves, slaps.

The emotional kinds—betrayal, rejection, bullying, mean teasing, hating, excluding, undermining, ridiculing, and on it goes—all the blows that do lasting harm.

Clare at her seventh-grade field trip riding her bumper car right into a wall and breaking her nose. The call: your daughter accelerated for reasons we don't understand and rammed right into the wall with such velocity that she broke her nose, dislocated her shoulder, and the bruises on her face have already started to bloom. Could you come get her?

Before that: the umbilical cord wrapped around her neck tightening each time I pushed.

At four, falling out of the loosely screened window of our friend's house into the wading pool that just happened to be full of water and cushioned the impact. And later when she had left home and gone to South America and fell again, a repeated theme this falling, this time off a balcony onto the patio below that shattered her arm. Why can I tell you about these? Because she survived? Because they didn't mar her life or face or body irreparably? Because the damage was physical rather than emotional and the scars haven't altered her beauty? Because I didn't push her out the window or drive her into the wall? It was my body she was inside, my pushing which caused the tightening of the cord—yet it was beyond my control, and in the end, she suffered no lasting harm.

My first real experience of the way our lives were intertwined. What makes writing about my children potentially harmful? What has stopped me in the past? What kinds of stories won't I tell and why?

Hurt

Why haven't I written about when my son was a little boy, not even two years old, and he took my neighbor's son's hand and walked toward the back-porch steps? Lynne and her two sons lived across the alley from our house and the three little boys played together in our sandbox or the swing set. Lynne and I would stand outside together in my stamp-sized yard talking while the boys did what little boys did—push dump trucks, dig holes. Her youngest, Lyle, and my David settled into an easy largely nonverbal friendship. But one day when they were holding hands, Lynne told her son *to stop it* in an alarmed voice and knocked her son's arm away from my son. Both boys looked confused—I don't think either one of them knew how such a simple gesture of friendship could be wrong. But it was clear from Lynne's voice and actions that she thought something was wrong. David walked over to my side and Lynne took her boys and went inside their house and nothing was ever the same again.

This cloud of wrong descending upon our little alley troubled me more than the squabbles my daughter occasionally had with girls in the neighborhood, even when Stacey nearly ruined her sleepover birthday party by demanding to go home in the middle of it. Why? Well, as disappointing as Stacey's behavior was, it could be named—she was homesick, not ready to spend the night elsewhere and it had little to do with Clare. David couldn't name what had happened when Lynne swatted Lyle's hand away from his, he could only feel some vague sense that what the boys were doing was deemed wrong. What was it and why? Being affectionate? Being friends? How are these wrong? We see girls walking hand in hand all the time and think nothing of it. But boys—well, that's another matter. David and Lyle were too young to process what had happened. I wasn't too young, I was just stunned. Why did Lynne react the way she did and why didn't I? A whole world of difference opened between us on the opposite sides of our shabby alley in Morgantown, West Virginia.

Her response to seeing her *boy* hold another *boy's* hand was burrowed so deep it became instinctual. As a mother, Lynne felt it her duty to nip what she considered feminized behavior in the bud. What a boy is and isn't was clear to Lynne, not something she questioned, not something to be shaped by Lyle himself.

What did she fear and why didn't I? Was I not performing my maternal duty? Lynne feared that her boy would appear girly and that would make him vulnerable to attacks by others. Complying with gender conventions is a kind of protection, then, a smooth surface that allows one to move through the world unharmed. Whereas bucking gender conventions will invite ridicule, exclusion, bullying, and perhaps worse. She did not think about the costs of depriving her boy of his natural inclinations for showing affection to another boy—that meant nothing compared to the danger he might be in if he did not channel his emotions into acceptable behavior.

A lesson in stunting the flow of affection in boys. A lesson in how shame starts early. A lesson in how the sorting starts young. A lesson in the role mothers play. And yet, I never wrote about it until now.

I doubt David remembers the incident. He might not even remember Lyle. But did the incident affect him unknowingly? It affected me. I don't know what David thought or felt when Lyle dropped his hand. He probably went on with his day. But I didn't. There was harm in Lynne's behavior toward our boys. Small though it was, it foretold other harms that were waiting, that would descend upon David and I didn't think there was much I could do about it. And while Clare's nose healed, I didn't know if David's sense of self, his inner happiness and confidence, would do as well with the battering and breakage that was coming. The harm went deeper, the cracks and breakages would run inside where no one could see them. And I felt helpless before this world of hurt.

Detection

Hurt and harm, these are my key words, as a writer, as a mother. Try to do neither. Know you may fail. There are some things you don't do as a writer, there are some things you don't do as a mother, even if others do. No one hands you an all-purpose writer's manual or a how-to guide when you become a mother. You look around and see what others are doing and decide whether that is a road you want to travel. You decide what is most important *to you*, what you can live with and what you can't. In other words, you decide based on *your character*. I suppose you decide based on the person you want to be.

In the field of creative nonfiction, writing about others is a hot topic. Each year at the Association of Writers & Writing Programs annual conference, where some variation of the subject is being discussed, the rooms are always full. Advice is handed out, guidelines are established, questions are answered. Nevertheless, the topic is never exhausted, and never retired, such is the anxiety of writers writing about their lives, which inevitably entails writing about others who largely did not ask to be written about and who might be hurt and harmed by being written about. It's a conundrum at the dark heart of the genre.

Writing about children, specifically one's own children, is an even more vexed problem. What might fly about writing about one's parents or ex-husband or former teacher, all adults who can respond in a variety of ways including breaking off the relationship, don't apply to a child who might still be dependent upon the writer-mother. Some writers argue that their child gave consent. But what can consent mean when it is given by a young person too inexperienced to know what the costs of being written about might be? And how many children will struggle refusing a mother and end up capitulating against their own best interests? No, the consent of children is suspect, and parents should see that and not put their children in an untenable position.

I remember when Julie Myerson published *The Lost Child* chronicling her son's drug addiction. Her son condemned the book and a public debate ensued: is it inappropriate and even harmful (there's that word) to expose the private lives of minors? It must be noted that the private life being exposed in these cases are always rife with difficulty. She wasn't writing about her child's triumphs. She was writing about a painful chapter in his young life, one he might like to keep to himself and not have follow him wherever he went, and his mother's justification that airing his story might help others was no solace or meaningful rationale *to him.* And yet in the debate, writers say with relish that *everyone* is fair game for a writer. No one is off limits for the writer. And the story is the thing—everything must be sacrificed for the story to be realized.

Writers hear these kinds of pearls of wisdom trotted out all the time to justify whatever must be done to bring a story to light. They're often used as a battering ram to suggest to a writer who is wavering about using certain material that they aren't really writers, they lack the courage and boldness necessary to be a writer. A real writer will make the selfish, difficult choice because they answer to a higher purpose.

I've known writers who knew they were causing their children pain by writing about them—the material was unflattering, shattering even—and they did it anyway. They believed in the worth of the story. Later they were baffled by the damage that had been done in their relationship with their child, a damage that couldn't be mended.

Some writers say that they'll write about their children up until the age of ten. After that, the story is no longer theirs—it belongs to their child. That feels a little arbitrary to me. Some things happened to me before the age of ten, and I would not have liked my mother writing about it as if it was her story. That said, I'm the first to acknowledge how what happens to my children in some sense happens to me. It's hard to draw a strict line between whose story it is.

For example, I was abused when I was in the second grade. I didn't tell my mother, but if I had told her, what happened to me was now something that happened to her. How did she feel, what should she do: this material would have been something she felt she wanted to write about because it mattered, and yet, to do that she would have exposed a painful incident in my life, and I would not have wanted her to do that. After all, I didn't tell her in the first place, I kept it a secret, a secret for a very long time.

As a writer, I've tried to burrow my way through the complications and come to conclusions that are right for me. And *for me* my ambition is to arrive at the end of my life and have my children think I've done them no harm through my writing. I'm like the guy on the beach with a metal detector combing the sand—looking for anything that is mine to tell.

Prayer

You could say I lack the requisite ambition to get very far in this writing business. It certainly is true that I don't believe that what I write warrants the sacrifice of my children. I began with the notion that how we decide who we are as writers comes down to our character and who we want to be. I don't want to be known as that writer who sold out her son for a measly day in the sun. Or for a *sum*. That doesn't mean I don't want to write works that last—I unfailingly do, but when I think of the writing I aspire to, Elizabeth Bishop's *In the Waiting Room* or Sylvia Plath's *Ariel* pops up. Or closer to my generic home, Joan Didion's *Blue Nights* about the death of her daughter. All writings born of the personal that have transmuted its potential to do harm into gold. Perhaps I've been too cautious, burned by being the child of parents who did a great deal of harm, and then later chastened by examples of writers whose writing hurt their children and fell far short of gold. It has been crucial to me that I not repeat the history of harm I had been born into. Have I over-compensated?

Surveying what I have written I see that my children rarely appear. David is prominent in only one essay called *Impromptu Mourner* published in a small Unitarian magazine. He was seven years old at the time and sometimes didn't come home for dinner. Usually one of us went looking for him and dragged him home. But this evening, a cool one in November, we couldn't find him, and we sat down for dinner in the dark without him. Eventually he wandered in hungry. When I asked him where he had been, he told quite the story. Our neighbor Sara Gifford, whose husband Roger had died that fall, snagged David on his way home and recruited him to help her bury Roger's ashes in her backyard next to the ashes of their dog. David dug the hole and threw the dirt over the box and then she took his hand and they said the Lord's Prayer, only David didn't know it. Later she came over to berate me about the inadequacy of David's religious training.

I did not say but I wrote—*Knowing how to feel in desperately sad situations and how to comfort those in need of comforting happens surprisingly early in life for some, and for some a lifetime isn't enough time to learn. David knew how to feel from the beginning. He may not have known the Lord's Prayer, but he knew churches aren't the only sacred places. He knew the most sacred place is the one he carried inside him and*

that he could stand with an elderly woman burying her husband and say
his own prayer.

Purse

The plane glided to the end of its flight, the seatbelt sign flashed off, the passengers righted themselves and crowded into the aisles. Seated by the window, with no inclination to hurl myself into the thoroughfare, I had a thought that often comes to me: people are inexplicable. Everyone knows that when the plane halts there's an idle minute while the exit ramp is hooked up and the doors open. If in the meantime you insist on standing up, you have to slump not to bang your head on the storage bins above, or else shove into the aisle, where flesh is pressed, where you feel claustrophobic and faint, because the air stops moving when the plane does. Far better to stay put, glance out the window at the weather, or read for a moment or two—which is what I did, sitting back to enjoy *David Copperfield*, more than a little comforted by a sense that I was displaying a wise philosophy of life. David's nemesis, Miss Murdstone, had herself just arrived by coach: "When she paid the coachman she took her money out of a hard steel purse, and she kept the purse in a very jail of a bag which hung upon her arm by a heavy chain, and shut up like a bite. I had never, at that time, seen such a metallic lady altogether as Miss Murdstone was."

The woman in the berth behind me did not see things the same way I did. She pulled herself to her feet, grunting as her seat cushion gave out a little sigh. She bent forward over the back of my seat, with no room to maneuver and at just such an angle that her big white leather bag, a purse of overnight proportions, with side flaps and a large gold clasp like a lion's head, roaming loose on a shoulder strap, rammed repeatedly into my neck. I leaned forward to avoid it, but I was boxed in between the window, the seats in front, and the folks slumping on my right. I wanted to whack the woman with my *David Copperfield*, but instead I asked myself a large question: whence came the purse? Surely naked Eve, striding through the Garden of Eden, had no need for one. She didn't require lipstick or mirror, keys or breath mints, painkillers, Lifesavers. No need for a wallet fat with credit cards and picture IDs; she didn't drive, didn't vote, and didn't owe money. But after the Fall, when death came into the world, she must have accessorized her shame with the purse, fruit of the tree of knowledge.[2]

This was the progenitor of the beast attacking my neck, a purse of such extravagant capacity that anything might have been folded inside it and locked away. It was like a motor home. I could see the woman at work, parking it in the top drawer of her filing cabinet. She seemed unaware that her accoutrement, more weapon than accessory, was slapping me senseless. I began to connect certain observations and draw conclusions. Women who, despite foreknowledge, rush headlong into the aisle and there sag against others who have unwittingly been cast as props in their drama—such women carry grotesquely large purses whose battering-ram potential they deny while deploying it against those who are more placid. I'd call them *women who lead with their purses.* They pay no attention to the damage they inflict upon innocent bystanders, and it's clear that this attitude, the attitude of *not noticing,* is passive-aggressive. Such women have been taught to deny their hostilities, their impatience. They would never thump someone on the head—but their purses would. Like the one at my neck. It was a tricky appendage; it moved when she moved, and yet it couldn't be said to be her. *The purse did it,* her subconscious was saying, *not me.*

Not all purses are aggressive and predatory. Take my childless Aunt Virgie. When I was a girl, she seemed already old, though she was not so old. She dyed her hair silver, but it seemed blue next to her soft pink baby's skin. She always wore a strand of pearls, of moderate length—not a choker and not a long loopy necklace—with matching studs in her ears. And of course, her purse. She carried one kind only, year after year, black and rectangular, hung from a short strap. She must have purchased them in bulk. The purse went everywhere Aunt Virgie went, and she never set it down. She stood with it resting on her hip, the way

---

2 Sometime after this flight, I learned that the Greeks carried small linen bags decorated with embroidery, and the Crusaders carried coins for the poor in alms bags, later enlarged to accommodate a prayer book. Until the pocket was introduced, it was men who had purses. They were in charge of finance, and they controlled currency. There must have been the exceptional woman who needed to keep a key or letter safe, but on the whole, history shows that women took up what men had vacated. By the early nineteenth century, women were clasping demure reticules.

mothers balance babies. When she shifted her weight, the purse shifted. When I hugged her hello and goodbye, I felt it come between us. Once I managed to look inside her purse, hoping to find illicit love letters, a velvet jewel case full of precious gems, and a silver flask of whiskey. Instead there was a small pillbox with tiny pills for her heart, a scented handkerchief, and a tube of worn-down ruby lipstick.

Unlike Aunt Virgie, my mother had many types of purses. She kept them lined up neatly on two shelves in her closet. When I opened the door, I used to shiver, for it seemed a bank vault. The smell was of freshly minted money. All the purses were in perfect condition. My mother never used one exclusively, for purses were like shoes, selected to match outfits. She had summer purses in pastels and white, in canvas and straw weaves. She had autumnal greens and browns, winter items of black patent leather, jaunty spring navys and hopeful light blues. She had evening purses beaded and studded, sequined and gilded, shoulder bags and clutch bags, and the one I remember most vividly—an alligator bag with matching shoes. This was the Cadillac of purses. It was square, with little gold legs so it could sit upright. Sleek and shiny, the skin stretched tight, without ripples or bubbles or give. It was almost airtight, and working the clasp took real strength. She seldom carried it, but when chosen it was slung from her lower arm, held stiffly away from the body, as if it might hurt her. She most often brought it when she attended meetings of an official nature at which she felt a need to be armed. The alligator purse commanded respect, opened doors, and quieted a room of chattering female voices.

At last there were signs—a flickering about the eyes—that the woman had caught a glimpse of my head, orphan wisps of hair poking out from behind her bag. Would she apologize? No, she would not. She fixed me with a look that said, *I'm not responsible for any wrongs committed. Purses will act out when one isn't watching, and they don't always behave wisely or well.* She was staring at my own purse, a limp woven affair with two thin floppy straps.

It is one of the peculiarities of my history that all of my purses have been gifts from my mother. She often asked me how a particular purse was doing. They hang from hooks in my closet, forlorn, a frame of mind very different from my mother's purses.

The first one came the Christmas I was twelve. From the shape of the package I judged it might be a music box that played a memorable theme. When I tore off the wrapping paper and lifted the lid of the box to find a green suede purse with a gold latch in the shape of a miniature horseshoe, I was mystified, for I had never spoken of purses. What a waste of a horseshoe, I thought, intending to pry it off.

I know a woman who, though reckless and personally unanchored, is fanatically particular and organized when it comes to purses. Last summer she lived out of her car, or rather her purse. She had no idea where she'd spend the night, what direction her whims might take her, but she knew where her belongings were. She had developed the art of the homeless; she improvised her world from what was immediately hers. In the purse she found her most concentrated and perfect expression.

One day she hauled it onto the bench between us for inspection. "Look," she said, "it has compartments. "Here I put bug spray, lip gloss, that sort of thing, first aid and repair." Another compartment contained the wallet, itself a finely tuned system, and her cigarettes and lighter. Demonstrating the rapidity with which she could locate any item, she said, "I can't stand having to reach into a bag and fish around for a cigarette. I always know exactly where it is and can reach it immediately." Her cigarette case had a compartment for her lighter, and after she lit her cigarette, she replaced the lighter. Her wallet was similarly constructed—two chambers, one for pennies, one for other change, two billfolds, one for singles and one for all else. The underside of the flap had slots for pens, a little toothbrush, and a flashlight. "See, everything has a place. When I'm done with a thing, I put it back where it belongs. I always know where to look." There was a place for her checkbook and pen, stamps, and two card files, the first for the most frequently used, which could be folded out, and the other for the less frequently used.

Lighting a cigarette, she picked up my purse, the woven straw affair my mother had meant for the beach, and laughed—"You call this a purse?" There are no inner compartments or pockets. Everything jumbles together, and it is, as she pointed out, impossible to find anything. I rarely know what exactly is in my purse, having forgotten what I earlier threw in. It is always sprawling open, spilling its contents.

I told her, "I like to clear my mind of such knowledge—the knowledge of what fills my purse."

She didn't buy this for a second. "How much brain space can it take to remember what's in your purse?"

I said, "I have to conserve what there is for larger questions."

"You have no system," she moaned. She grabbed my wallet. Here I wad bills in the change compartment, mixed in with the coins. Each time I buy something, I have to pull out all the money to see what I have. The billfold ripped apart years ago. This acceptance of disrepair distressed my friend, but she was truly sickened by the state of my cards. All of them, and there was quite a pile, are smashed into one pocket, in what I think of as a free-spirited fashion. I have to file through them until I find the desired one.

I told her, "If I pay attention to my purse, then I will belong to it. I don't want to belong to my purse." I have no desire to be the first off the plane, to wear the accessories of command, no desire to become a woman with a purse. My purse will not be the calm in the wake of catastrophe. I want to be like Eve, striding naked through the world with no need to house her possessions. I don't want the illusion of control. If my life is a mess, the perfection of my purse won't fix it. My purse will not speak of me when I'm gone, nor satisfy my yearnings.

Some women believe their purses are human, and it is to their purses that interesting things happen. Or so I was thinking when I woke up on the plane and saw that the aisles had cleared. I took my purse in hand, found the exit, and with wandering steps took my solitary way out into the open air.

Enough

I am lying awake in an unfamiliar bed, thinking about success. It is not a king-size bed, nor a queen-size bed, but a double, shared with my husband in a two-room cottage of four hundred square feet that I call the Hut. I am lying here, thinking about success, because I have left my home and driven across the country to take up a semester's residence as the Mary Routt Chair in Writing at Scripps College, one of the Claremont Colleges. It is the bottom hour of the night, and ahead of me lies the long ascent of time toward morning.

The Hut sits a few blocks north of another one of the Claremont Colleges, Pomona, where thirty years ago I was an undergraduate. Much has changed in Claremont since then, yet much remains the same. Old halls have been torn down, replaced by modern structures, yet the streets still carry the thick smell of eucalyptus. Once I earned my degree at Pomona, I moved on to a working life, to commutes on subway and bus, to corporate work and housecleaning, to graduate school, marriage and children, teaching and writing. I didn't envision coming back. And yet this return has felt necessary, even preordained, as if the time for a reckoning has come.

By many measures my return is a sign of success. I have done enough of what I set out to do—be a writer and a professor— to warrant selection to this named position. But I do not feel triumphant. No wreath of bay circles my crown. Just the opposite: I feel as if I'm lying on a bed of nails. Wandering the old campus gardens and courtyards, I meet my younger self, who doesn't give me a congratulatory wave, passing by on her way to an important appointment. Instead she sits down beside me on the bench under the wisteria and stares into my face, assessing what I have become. Her eyes darken with disappointment. She finds me wanting. *What happened?* she asks. *I thought you would amount to so much more. I thought there would be so much more of you. It isn't enough,* she says.

How slender she is, yet filled with expectation! Could I ever have been so young and fierce and yet so innocent? How her eyes brim with yearning! She's sure she's going to do something great with her life; no obstacle will derail her. *Little angel,* I say, *what did you expect of me, and why are you so disappointed?* It's true that I haven't written the great American novel, but haven't I done enough?

In the deep hull of the night I lie, first in a sweat and then in a chill. There is no in-between; it's always from one extreme straight to the other. When I can't sleep, like now, I could get up, move to the little kitchen and living room. I could take care of tasks. I could dust, sew on a missing button. I could make a sandwich, have a glass of wine. But I never get up. I lie in bed and brood, as if I'm bound to the headboard. What keeps me tied here? Maybe I'm doing emotional homework that can't be done anywhere else—an assignment on the subject of what has passed and what is coming. They say that insomnia strikes women most, especially women of my age. My women friends are cool in the heat of the day, unflappable in the midst of breakdown and catastrophe, but at night their emotions pour forth and flood the bed.

It is not enough to be a success. Success is not enough because there's always someone more successful. I rarely compare myself to someone who has achieved less. I notice the person ahead of me, not the person behind. I'm focused on the one who won the prize and forget about the people who were passed over. I ask myself how many among us are where we want to be, who we want to be—as if I could argue my way out of the night. But there's always somewhere we want to get, something more we need to accomplish, something to fix. Such dissatisfaction is good, keeps us moving forward. But too much self-criticism can mist our compass, make us lose our bearings. When will the tallying end, this measuring of myself against every other, this measuring myself against myself, this feeling of finding myself wanting?

I listen to the falling footsteps on rasping gravel of deep-night strangers who cut through the alley that runs fifteen feet beyond the bedroom wall. Last night my good friend sent me an email because she was lying awake in bed thinking how different her life was from the very publicly successful Elena Kagan's. Of late the news has been full of her confirmation to the Supreme Court. (I wonder how many other women of my generation are lying awake tonight, thinking about that place of marble columns.) She is near to our age, the age of feminism's ascent, but for my friend the differences between Elena Kagan and herself are greater than the similarities:

No elite institutions for me. Who knows what any of that would have meant, but it was not my path; nor storied appointments in the highest-quality institutions, and now the honor of a lifetime. And I've had kids and am married. Elena Kagan? Nope. Can it be done? So could it have been different for me? I don't know, but I guess all of us who are 45–60 have been impacted by greater opportunity, but nothing like equal opportunity.

Can it be done? Can a woman excel at the highest professional level and devote herself to marriage and children? Or must she choose one or the other? My friend and I are the first women in our families to attempt the grand experiment—the first to go to graduate school, the first to attempt career and family.

Elena Kagan has come onto the national scene at a difficult point in my friend's struggle to juggle career and family life. There's isn't enough of her to go around. She is a capable and strong woman; still she cannot sufficiently manage her house, her sons' complicated lives, her marriage, the dog and cat, the doctors and dentists and plumbers, supervise homework, make and serve healthy meals, fulfill her teaching and service requirements at her place of employment, deliver papers at conferences, write books, have a social life, reply to emails and phone calls, exercise and keep herself in shape. It can't be done. I know because I've tried. Corners had to be cut, expectations left unmet. I had to decide whom to disappoint. I prioritized what *had* to be done and then felt bad about what I didn't do or did in a way that fell short of my own standards. Sometimes I felt I wasn't doing a good job at anything, and I wanted to throw in the towel. But I couldn't, and neither can my friend. We can't give up anything listed in our catalogue raisonné. Send back children? I don't think so. Nor do we want to. Give up job and retire to the home? I don't think so. Who will pay the mortgage, the bills? Think again. So my friend was in a low state, a state I recognized. She was asking why her life wasn't as successful as Elena Kagan's. What did she do wrong?

How should I respond? I could point out that my friend did nothing wrong, but made different choices. Unlike the Supreme Court justice, she didn't remain single and childless. She chose to negotiate her life with a spouse who had ambitions of his own. Will it make my friend feel better for me to say that Kagan can devote herself entirely to the demands of her work? To say there are choices we make and each has its price? Probably not.

I don't have the same desires my friend does, nor ambitions to ascend the judicial system. I do want whatever literary gift I have to bloom inside me, not to clot and curdle. But this shift of arenas brings no comfort. It doesn't make me feel better when I itemize the differences in circumstances between Virginia Woolf and me. There is that small matter of unfathomable greatness, hers, not mine. Genius, I'd say. Even if I had a room of my own and one hundred pounds a year with prewar prices and servants to clean my house and make my meals and gardeners to spray my roses, I would not have matched what she produced, or even come close. I would have found other ways to dither. Even if we had the exact same opportunities, I am not Virginia Woolf.

Success—there is some je ne sais quoi to it, isn't there? But, of course, that's finally not the point, or at least not for me. The point is that I wanted to take whatever gift I had and devote myself to it. Have I? I'm not sure. Maybe. I don't know. I can't be objective. I don't *feel* I have. I point to various reasons for why I haven't. Chief among them is the choice I made to have children, and not just that, but to raise my own children rather than hire someone to do the job for me. And money, the lack of it, plays a role, a rather large role. When you don't have money, you have to do most everything yourself. Whatever comes along that needs doing, you do it. Material conditions: they aren't the same for everyone. And it can drive a person crazy. Could I have been more successful if . . . ? Would I have been more successful if . . . ? I will never total it all. It's possible that I might have accomplished less than I have and been free from disappointment. We make choices. We don't know in advance the consequences of those choices, how the story will turn out. No doubt, whatever we hope to achieve will be harder than we ever imagined. It's called risk-taking.

Must a woman choose, I've wondered? Yes, unless she wants to be torn asunder by competing demands and desires. The women writers I loved when young—Emily Brontë, Jane Austen, George Eliot, Virginia Woolf, Willa Cather, Emily Dickinson, Edith Wharton—did not have children, and I wondered why. The answer I provided was that they devoted themselves to writing. Other possible answers exist, but I interpreted their childlessness as a necessary refusal in order to embrace their writing. When I rode the bus to school in ninth grade, I sat next to Susan, who spent most of the ride inking out names for children she dreamed of having when she grew up. She wanted a large family, and the lists filled pages of her notebook. Sitting on the ripped vinyl seat, looking out the window at the fields of Pennsylvania corn, I scribbled the titles of books I hoped to write. Most of my girlfriends aspired to a life fulfilled through marriage and children. When I was that schoolgirl, I fantasized about arranging my life to serve my writing. I dreamed of a life that would begin and end in my solitary bed, with just enough room for myself, a book, and a writing pad.

In one of my history's ironic twists, I did not arrange my life along the solitary lines I envisioned at fifteen. I chose to share a bed. Among my friends, I was the first to marry, and I had my first child in graduate school. My life has been more haphazard than I imagined, and all my boundaries have been overrun. I've tried to do too much, with certain predictable results. Picture a woman whipping up a soufflé while vacuuming the living room where a baby bounces in the doorway with the phone ringing in the background and someone is knocking on the door and a notebook lies open on the counter with a pen lying abandoned in the crease. That would be me. Oh, and add a stack of student papers that need to be graded and another stack of books I'm teaching and a dog and three cats. Maybe a few plants capsized on a bookshelf.

It has been impossible to know with certainty what would feed me, what would make my writing rich, what would make my life rich, and so I have followed my instincts. My inclinations have been to have children, a complicated home life, a career and writing life, rather than not to try. I might come to ruin by this method, but an orderly life has not been for me. I couldn't see myself with a writing life but no children, or a life with children but no writing. I rushed into chaos and possible catastrophe, and I just kept going. Perhaps this has meant that I have not been as successful at any one function as I might have been if I had harnessed all my energies to one task.

I've gotten myself into quite a tangle tonight, a tangle of sheets and second guesses. The sirens on Foothill Boulevard, which sound all night though there are no hospitals nearby, call me toward a rocky shore. The truth is, I don't fit the category of the middle-aged woman who is nostalgic for those golden years when sleep was a hammock stretched between two weeping willows. I don't remember a time when I slept contentedly. I've always been at least two people—the woman who was disappointed and the woman who had had enough of disappointment—and the two of them never fit happily in the same bed.

The tallying of who I was and who I wasn't began in high school, if not before. In high school the fear of disappointing kept me awake, and in particular the fear of disappointing Mrs. Bierds, who taught French and Latin, the two languages I was studying to graduate from Moravian Seminary for Girls. I had the same teacher for both, for all four years, two hours a day, five days a week. Now, watching the blades of the fan go round and round trying to move the stale air around our little box, I calculate how many hours that adds up to. Roughly speaking, I was a captive of Mrs. Bierds's classroom for 1,360 hours of my life.

Mrs. Bierds was all of five feet on tippy toe, and wore navy blue suits with a blouse white as a celestial cloud, whose cuffs and bib ruffled fulsomely. The ruffles aside, Mrs. Bierds was altogether a flesh-and-blood creature whose high heels clicked with military precision on the linoleum up and down the rows of girls bent over their books. I'd startle to attention when her green felt pointer tapped on my desk to indicate it was my turn to translate. Surprised anew at her beak of a nose, I'd make a feeble stab at translating some innocuous sentence: *Je voudrais aller a la danse mais je n'ais pas de chaussures.* I hated to disappoint Mrs. Bierds. No, that's not right—I couldn't *bear* to disappoint her. I couldn't bear to see her opinion of me slide down the thin slope of her nose with her glasses. When I made a mistake, her blue eyes went all liquid behind her glasses, and her green felt pointer drooped listlessly by her side, as if she had forgotten where she was and couldn't go on. I had dealt her a terrible blow and it was only 9:20 on a mundane Monday morning with Latin to follow at 10:00.

Mrs. Bierds, a childless widow, had pinned her hopes on me for reasons that were incomprehensible at the time, and was happy with nothing less than perfection. *Tout le temps!* The night before a quiz, it was not enough to study hard and then shut the book, thinking, *I did the best I could, no one could ask for more,* and fall into a deep sleep. No, I lay awake, caressing each vocabulary word, a jeweled egg, while worrying that I had left a slip of learning unfinished. Catastrophe should have been tattooed across my ceiling, for there was never a shortage of disasters to be imagined. I was a good student of French and Latin, but I was advanced in Disasters.

I'm not sure when it hit me forcefully that I was flawed, essentially flawed, and no regime of self-improvement would change that, but I'm sure my mother had something to do with it. Mrs. Bierds was just a stand-in. My mother did a good job convincing me I was doomed to disappoint, that everything about me required a complete renovation, though back in high school I didn't realize that I would disappoint myself more than anyone else. (That took decades to discover.) I considered having a T-shirt made that said *I am a deeply disappointing person* because I felt a duty to warn people, to push them away in case they didn't see my flaws and became attached to me. Any success took me by surprise and seemed a mistake. I waited for the correction to follow—I'd be stripped of the part in the play, the teacher would recalculate my A, the SATs would be rescored, the boy would come to his senses and dump me, the college acceptance revoked. Nothing seemed too small to worry about. I envisioned a grand tribunal sitting in golden chairs in the night sky, glaring down through my windows and judging me. The tribunal was made up of ancient women with white hair falling past their shoulders to their knees, who would ask in hushed voices: *What did you do today? What do you plan on doing tomorrow? Will it be enough?*

Enough. A word like a high mountain I can't cross to see what's on the other side—perchance a valley of milk and honey where every woman has plenty of what she needs and what she wants and knows she has reached her paradise. She's satisfied—she doesn't hanker after what hasn't been done. Enough. What's enough for me may not be enough for you. I may have wanted to tell my mother and a whole line of mother substitutes that I'd *done enough*, but I didn't because I knew my mother would say, *No, you haven't* and I wasn't sure that she wasn't right. *Enough* can't be precisely measured, precisely stated because it's part of an emotional economy. One has to guess, make an estimate. How many hours of work is enough to consider myself productive? How much love is enough to feel loved? How many kisses are enough to feel kissed? How much money is enough to feel secure? Whatever scheme of measurement used, the evidence suggests it is the rare woman who has enough of anything, who doesn't want more money, more love, more time, more kisses. And in my world it is the rare woman who doesn't taunt herself because she hasn't accomplished enough, who isn't lying awake at night making yet another tally.

I'm lying in bed thinking about my mother, and now the room is boiling. When will the temperature drop and a breeze begin to bang the eucalyptus branch against the window? All roads lead back to my mother. Only one female friend in her set, a widow, held a job, even though most of them were college educated, some better educated than the husbands, like my mother, who graduated from Wellesley. She never contemplated working, nor wanted her daughters to have a career. My young students can't imagine the stark landscape women of my generation faced, or the generations before mine. When I tell them I had only one female professor in college, they think I'm talking about a time around the Civil War. They don't understand how the world was divided, like laundering darks and lights, and not so long ago. You absolutely had to separate the loads—you couldn't find local examples of women who were making something of themselves professionally and being a mother. My mother taught me many things. Some of them I didn't want to learn, most of them did not prepare me to enter a professional world run by men, and many I'd like to rid myself of and can't, for they are more easily learned than unlearned. She taught me how to turn knives outward in a proper table setting, how to fold a napkin, which fork is the salad fork, how to have a headache, how to talk to salespersons and waitresses and others who aren't at your station, how to write a thank-you note, how to play solitaire, how to answer the phone in a frightfully cheerful voice when a minute ago you were having a humdinger of a fight with a family member, how to appear in control and poised when your insides are crumbling, how to be in a room without making it dirty, how to hand-wash delicate items, how to garnish a dish, how to flatter a man without even trying, how to conduct a conversation so that one's interlocutor feels important, how to appear to listen when you don't, how to suffer others' superiority, how to read a book as if your life depended on it, how to downplay your own intelligence so effectively you no longer think you are intelligent, how to defer to others, how to turn your anger inward, how to clean when you are unhappy, how to make a bed with hospital corners, how to stay silent about what you want, how to be charming in social situations in a perfectly shallow way, how to feel being female closed more doors than it opened. Of these, learning how to read a book may be the best lesson she taught me. I want to leave my mark on a room once I leave it—the verdict is out on whether I've learned that or not.

I'm remembering a nightmare, an anxiety dream about arriving at a final exam without a pencil or a blue book. Only in my allegory, I'm riding my bike along a path that cuts through the woods when I encounter a famous writer. He is confident, assured, and oozing easy charm. He wears his success as if it's his birthright. Our bikes collide, and I am thrown into a large oak tree while he remains mysteriously upright and unscathed. While helping me up off the ground, instead of inquiring if I'm hurt, he asks: "What's your greatest accomplishment?" Brushing away the wing of hair that has fallen across my eyes and taking a deep breath, I lean into the microphone he has produced from his safari jacket and say, "Staying upright." He searches my face, now covered with dirt, and sees I mean it. He laughs and laughs, pedaling away rapidly. My bike is mangled, with flattened tires. I will have to walk the bike all the way home, listening to the wheels squeak.

I recall an awkward but real collision over lunch with two male senior colleagues my first year employed in my tenure track job. We were huddled in a poorly lit and uncomfortable booth at the restaurant constructed of dark pine that the older academics favored. I was picking at a spinach salad, the designated female lunch, while they were piling down the extra hot chili and roast beef sandwiches. They were reminiscing nostalgically about their uninterrupted path from college to graduate school to university job and so on through the usual promotions and leaves, but sensing that my path did not follow theirs, probably from a twitch in my right eye, had politely asked me about my trajectory. I nearly sprayed them with the lemon water I was sipping.

I rehearsed my path silently. How my family had advised me to enter secretarial school or marry a doctor, my detour after college into office work and cleaning other people's houses, the doctoral exams taken with morning sickness, my orals while nine months pregnant, the bed where I wrote my dissertation with a baby crawling over the pages, the lack of maternity leaves, the heart-wrenching negotiations with my spouse about whose career would be followed and the terrible trade-offs that followed for both of us.

Coming to the end of my silent reckoning, I blurted out, "No, that's not how my life has gone. I was having too much sex to focus so single-mindedly on my career." I don't know what possessed me: a desire to shock, a need to bring the female body of difference to bear upon this cozy fraternity? Everyone in the department knew I had two children under the age of four; it had been announced over loudspeakers. I was the first female faculty member hired with a family in place, referred to as the "new hire with family," as if it were a census category, or a rare and contagious disease. My colleagues looked at my stroller as if they had never seen such a vehicle before. They bent down to inspect its wheels, emitting *Ah* before scurrying back into their offices and closing the door. The career sphere and the domestic sphere had remained separate and uncontested in their lifetimes and governed by two different people.

Maybe the imp of darkness inside me made me speak. The effect of my answer, offered in loud, brazen, and defensive tones, made their forks freeze in midair. It was not the answer they expected or deserved. They expected to hear a story that tweaked in a minor way the plot outline of their story. But it was not. It was a new female kind of story and I could not tell it smoothly, could not weave it into theirs with calm confidence. And it was true the thing I said about sex, the sex thing, though by sex I meant something larger than the act of sex. I meant the consequences of being a sexual person, the children that issued forth, but something bigger still about growing up female and wanting a career, and wanting marriage and family, wanting everything and not knowing how to manage it all. I meant an exchange—uneven, fraught with history, with the ghosts of families past, with longings, his and mine, deferred, negotiated, and sometimes stunted.

Maybe it was the fighter within the deeply flawed person that spoke up in such an unruly way, just as I had spoken up against my mother. Something inside me fights for a view of myself that isn't so disappointing—a kind of inchoate anger rises up. I lie awake battling it out—who am I? Am I like some of the women at the pool where I swim who stand at the edge of an occupied lane, hesitating to ask the swimmer if she might join him. They've got their bathing caps pulled tight and their goggles ready to go, and yet they wait for someone to make room for them. Woman after woman stands for twenty minutes, until a breaking point is reached. Will she cave and return to the locker room or make a stand? Which is it going to be? If a woman hesitates to join a lane, what else does she hesitate before and with what consequences?

When my daughter was little she was obsessed with saving someone or something from disaster. I'd say in a joking manner, "I'm a disaster, why don't you save me?" She'd say in the most earnest voice, "Mommy, I want to be useful." She'd plot imperiled situations with her dolls—a grease fire on one of the burners sputtering out of control and her doll house exploding in flames. She'd rush in to save the day, carrying her dolls to safety. Then she'd open her doctor's bag, apply cold compresses to the burns, and bandage heads. She wanted to be a firefighter, and one Christmas asked for the uniform. Her uncle asked her what she wanted to be when she grew up. She, of course, said a firefighter. He laughed. "But dear girl," he said, "girls can't be firefighters. Only men." And like the resourceful child she was, she did not lay down her dream at his feet in grief. She looked at him the way I used to look when I was younger—fierce in her determination not to be thwarted. She's grown up now and while she has not joined the Firefighters of America, she is a nurse who works in the burn unit. Her hands have lost none of their youthful ability to radiate heat. She does not spend much of her time worrying about whether she is successful or not since her successes are often measured in lives saved or lost, and despite her best efforts, some of her patients die. She asks herself if she is being of use.

I remember one morning when I didn't want to get up. I hadn't slept much. She came into the bedroom and said, "Mommy, it's time to get up." Her voice was not scolding or disappointed. She was calm and matter-of-fact.

I said, "Let me think about it."

To which she replied, "You have been thinking about it and you don't have much time left. It's time now."

She was right then and she's still right: it's time to get up. The garbage truck has come to empty the cans in the alley. The night's drifting thought ends, with no shore reached, no success in thinking through to some grand epiphany about success. I can't total it all. There's only beginning another day in which I will separate the darks from the lights, at the end of which I can say, *I did the best I could and that is not enough, that will never and always be not enough.* And lay me down again in the black shape of the night.

Inflammatory Questions

Inspired by Jenny Holzer's Inflammatory Essays

Was it in Mr. Hinderlie's class your junior year in high school, when you had to compose a story from scratch every night for three weeks, that you began to think you might be a writer? It felt like riding your horse without a saddle, your skin next to his. Why were you surprised by the full-throated ease of what came out of you?

You didn't want to be consoled, did you? But then no one ever consoled you, no one even tried, so that would be a stupid thing to want. Didn't you want to burn, to feel the chafe and the rub?

Or did it start years earlier in the sickbed when you had chicken pox and all you wanted to do was scratch? Wasn't it then, reading *Jane Eyre* and *Wuthering Heights,* propped up by pillows and looking out onto a landscape of swirling snow, that you felt them calling?

What in the world was Mr. Hinderlie thinking, assigning a story a day? Dinner finished quickly and you retreated to your room to begin what lay ahead

Was it in those early days in college when your typewriter vibrated on the desk, its powerful motor electrifying the dorm room? Can you say what impulse seized

Remember how you gathered each morning in high school waiting for the inner doors to the chapel to be unlocked? Remember your weird anticipation as you flowed in of you. What did lay ahead of you? There was no path to follow, just the open field of the page. Where did the shape of the sentences come from? Will you ever understand the voice that carried you to places you didn't know you had inside you? you to put your hands on the wizard device, to pump its keys and make an unknown thing upon the page? with the others to sit on one of the straight-backed chairs in two rows on either side of the center aisle. Remember how you wondered what the sermon's message of the day would be. To yearn is to seek something missing. What were you missing? Are you missing it still?

It didn't seem possible, did it, that you could be a writer, coming from a family of insurance salesmen, dentists, and pump inventors, who wanted no more for you than to marry a rich man? Marry, they said. Marry, they urged. Marry. But that was the last What held you back—the incredulousness of your family, or your own self-doubt, or were those one and the same? That self-doubt, started so long ago, hasn't changed much, has it? Your family's view of you travels with you wherever you go. How far would you have to go to be rid of it? When you are introduced at a reading, why do you think that person is someone other than you? Will you ever not feel, when you take the podium, that you have risen above your station? Why have you always thought of yourself as a secondary subject, a minor character on stage, the maid

thing on your
mind, wasn't it?

When you found
your mother's
suitcase in the
crawl space, why
did you open it?
Did you think
there were
secrets inside
that your
mother didn't
want you to
find? Was that
the first
transgression of
the rule that we
should respect
what belongs to
others? Didn't
you know there
was something
wrong about
opening it?

Was opening
your mother's
suitcase your
first act as a
writer? Why did
you have to
know what was
inside? And did
you really think
you could stuff
what you found
back in? Didn't
you know your
mother's suitcase
was like
Pandora's box?

carrying platters
of food?

Once opened,
never closed.
Why do you
return—to open
the suitcase over
and over? Do
some wounds
refuse to be
worked through
once and for all?
Why do you want
to relive the
tumble of little
photographs
documenting
your mother's
and sisters'
happiness,
spilling out on
the cold cement
floor, feel your
heart rise up at
the image before
you?

Could Professor
K. have been
deluded about
your talent all
those years ago,
and might you
have built your
life on his
mistake? What if
he simply
wanted to sleep

On Keats'
gravestone: *Here
lies one whose
name was writ in
water.* Do others
wonder if what
they've written
will last? Or are
they content to
write, publish,

Is it possible to
tell true talent
from all the false
pretenders? And
if it does matter,
how does it
matter, and when
will the true
sorting take
place?

with you, and it had nothing to do with your hidden greatness? Can you separate desire from discernment?

and do it all again?

You didn't want to be consoled, did you? But then no one ever consoled you, no one even tried, so that would be a stupid thing to want. Didn't you want to burn, to feel the chafe and the rub?

What in the world was Mr. Hinderlie thinking, assigning a story a day? Dinner finished quickly and you retreated to your room to begin what lay ahead of you. What did lay ahead of you? There was no path to follow, just the open field of the page. Where did the shape of the sentences come from? Will you ever understand the voice that carried you to places you didn't know you had inside you?

Could Professor K. have been deluded about your talent all those years ago, and might you have built your life on his mistake? What if he simply wanted to sleep with you, and it had nothing to do with your hidden greatness? Can you separate desire from discernment?

Was it in those early days in

Or did it start years earlier in

Was it in Mr. Hinderlie's class

college when
your typewriter
vibrated on the
desk, its
powerful engine
electrifying the
dorm room? Can
you say what
impulse seized
you to put your
hands on the
wizard device, to
pump its keys
and make an
unknown thing
upon the page?

the sickbed when
you had chicken
pox and all you
wanted to do
was scratch?
Wasn't it then,
reading *Jane
Eyre* and
*Wuthering
Heights,* propped
up by pillows
and looking out
onto a landscape
of swirling
snow, that you
felt them
calling?

your junior year
in high school,
when you had to
compose a story
from scratch
every night for
three weeks, that
you began to
think you might
be a writer? It
felt like riding
your horse
without a saddle,
your skin next to
his. Why were
you surprised by
the full-throated
ease of what came
out of you?

When you are
introduced at a
reading, why do
you think that
person is
someone other
than you? Will
you ever not
feel, when you
take the podium,
that you have
risen above your
station? Why
have you always
thought of
yourself as a
secondary
subject, a minor
character on

Remember how
you gathered
each morning in
high school
waiting for the
inner doors to
the chapel to be
unlocked?
Remember your
weird
anticipation as
you flowed in
with the others
to sit on the
straight-backed
chairs in two
rows on either
side of the center
aisle?

When you found
your mother's
suitcase in the
crawl space, why
did you open it?
Did you think
there were
secrets inside that
your mother
didn't want you
to find? Was that
the first
transgression of
the rule that we
should respect
what belongs to
others? Didn't
you know there
was something

stage, the maid
carrying platters
of food?

What held you
back—the
incredulousness
of your family,
or your own
self-doubt, or
were those one
and the same?
That self-doubt,
started so long
ago, hasn't
changed much,
has it? Your
family's view of
you travels with
you wherever
you go. How far
would you have
to go to be rid of
it?

On Keats'
gravestone: *Here
lies one whose
name was writ in
water.* Do others
wonder if what
they've written
will last? Or are
they content to
write, publish,
and do it all
again?

Could Professor
K. have been
deluded about
your talent all
those years ago,
and might you
have built your
life on his
mistake? What if
he simply wanted
to sleep with you,
and it had
nothing to do
with your hidden
greatness? Can
you separate
desire from
discernment?

wrong about
opening it?

What lay ahead
of you? There
was no path to
follow, just the
open field of the
page. Why were
you surprised by
the full-throated
ease of what
came out of you?

It didn't seem
possible, did it,
that you could
be a writer,
coming from a
family of
insurance
salesmen,
dentists, and
pump inventors,
who wanted no
more for you
than to marry a
rich man?

Is it possible to
tell true talent
from all the false
pretenders? And
if it does matter,
how does it
matter, and when
will the true
sorting take
place?

Marry, they said.
Marry, they
urged. Marry.
But that was the
last thing on
your mind,
wasn't it?

Was opening
your mother's
suitcase your
first act as a
writer? Why did
you have to
know what was
inside? And did
you really think
you could stuff
what you found
back in? Didn't
you know your
mother's
suitcase was like
Pandora's box?

Once opened,
never closed.
Why do you
return—to open
the suitcase over
and over? Do
some wounds
refuse to be
worked through
once and for all?
Why do you
want to relive
the tumble of
little
photographs
documenting
your mother's
and sisters'
happiness,
spilling out on
the cold cement
floor, feel your
heart rise up at
the image before
you?

Remember how
you wondered
what the
sermon's message
of the day would
be? To yearn is to
seek something
missing. What
were you
missing? Are you
missing it still?

The Rejection

> They wait, when they should turn to journeys,
> They stiffen, when they should bend.
>
> —Louise Bogan, "Women"

I debated whether to go. The invitation to attend the reading arrived from a friend and colleague, the nicest invitation—written with old-school manners, simple but charming, sounding just the right note. Weighing the sweetness of the invitation and the opportunity, surely the last, to see and hear this poet in the flesh, I decided to go.

The poet had swung through town a few years before to launch a different book and on that occasion I had undergone a complicated line of thinking that arrived at a negative conclusion, a refusal, a demurral. I didn't want to put a face to the woman who had so memorably rejected me when I was a young guileless girl just out of college and sending my poems out for the first time as my professors had encouraged me to do. Encouraged is too mild a word to describe the push I felt to take the next step with my writing. I was ready, they said. I was not.

Something had changed since that earlier refusal and my current willingness to hear the poet. I'm on my way out of this place where I have taught and lived, I'm in the midst of a long goodbye, and since making the decision I've felt as if I'm looking at my time here through the eyes of the soon to be departed. I'm keeping a journal of my last "professional" days. Once you start such a project, it turns out topics arrive every day—professors from my past die, professors who I worked with here die, comparisons are made about changes in the profession, differences between my own education as a student and my experience as a teacher. And instead of turning away from opportunities like seeing the poet, an opportunity that I feared would reopen a wound I had with time healed, I now see through this different lens, the goodbye lens.

Seeing the poet is part of the reckoning I have undertaken— she's gotten all tangled up in the whys and wherefores of my life as a writer and a teacher. No doubt she'd be stunned to learn that she played any role at all in my life. I am a stranger, after all. And perhaps she just deserves a footnote. But she stands in for so many puzzling currents that eddy behind her that she's taken on water. Have I played a similar role as a teacher or editor for some stranger, did something I say lodge deep in their life?

I don't know what I expected. Up until minutes before I left my house, I thought I might bag it and stay home. I wavered. But I went; it was important now to look at what had happened and who it was who had written those words that like an arrow found the bull's eye of the target. The room was full of retired faculty who could still be counted on to show up at readings and concerts with a sprinkling of heads that were not gray or white or bald.

I thought she would be older. I thought the woman who rejected me decades ago, when I lived in Los Angeles in Echo Park on top of the hill overlooking Chavez Ravine where I could see and hear Dodger Stadium, was older. She sounded tired and bitter in the letter she wrote me rejecting my poem. How could someone as young as she must have been then sound that old and unkind? The poet wore her hair long, streaked silver, especially in the front, but still dark black. She caught it in a silver clip and the hair was thick and heavy on her back. Large and showy earrings, studded with diamonds, dangled dramatically from her ears. A white-and-black patterned scarf was tied ornately about her neck. She wore black jeans and a black jacket, not the baggy, waistless pants most of the other women wore. She held onto the drama and shape of her appearance, a beauty still, a woman who took pride in her beauty, protecting it, burnishing it, after a lifetime one could see of being invested in it, perhaps invested in it more than anything else, her passport.

Not what I expected. I thought she would be matronly, someone I would feel a world of difference from. Instead I felt more affinity with her than the other women who had assembled to listen. (*Say it! I felt a kinship.*) She struck me as someone who might have viewed, might still view, women as rivals, not as friends and confidantes, not as companions, but competitors for the spoils. For men, for position, for attention, for compliments, for praise, for publication. Wanting all eyes to be upon her. While she was no longer young, this need to be seen as a beauty, as the subject of appreciation, hadn't dimmed, or not much, though the sheen was streaked with melancholy, perhaps even a touch of remorse. She hadn't let her beauty go although she might be trying to do just that, I thought, listening to her read poems about the ruin of a great beautiful city. The poems spoke of white privilege and high culture, of a life lived abroad, of great art and seduction. She had spent time in this city, knew its language, returned to it many times, spent her happiest year living there, discovered her own beauty and sexuality there, memorably as a twelve-year-old who men whistled at in the streets, and older friends of her mother's became unnerved by her body in a bikini at the pool. She presented herself in these poems as a Lolita, aware of herself as a sexual object, and far from resisting that disposition, embracing it and thrilling to its supposed power. Her hands, with their large rings, gestured continuously throughout her reading. She was never still. She peered out to us over her eyeglasses perched halfway down her beautifully sloped nose.

She was nervous, but only her trembling voice and breathing gave her away. Her speaking voice, used to introduce the poems, and her reading voice were the same—for which I give her credit. She didn't affect that *poet's voice*, with its artificial rhythms and grandeur. Her lines did not lift toward the end or dip into hushed preciousness. Her poems were about sex and a city saturated with desire, where famous visitors discovered their appetites, where she herself discovered herself as a seductress, an identity that seemed alive still. The poems were complicated, elegies to a city and to her former self, alive in these ruins. She reckoned with her age and her past. No longer that youthful slip of a girl, she could only come near her in these poems of re-creation. The poet wanted to both memorialize her and let her float downstream, like an Ophelia.

I remember the day I received the rejection. It was a Friday afternoon in autumn when the Santa Ana winds were blowing— those dry, hot winds that put one on edge, literary winds. Raymond Chandler wrote about them, and Joan Didion. The rejection came with the mail, of course, as they did before email took over the task, but like all rejections I was surprised by its arrival and unprepared to receive it. Rejection always comes at the wrong time. Is anyone ever prepared for it? Weeks earlier, perhaps months earlier I had sent out packets of poems to a variety of literary magazines I read. I frequented libraries and read the literary journals they carried and went to bookstores and stood for hours in the aisles reading the work. I had made a list of the journals I admired and carefully typed my submission letter and made my little packets of poems and my SASE and walked them to the post office. The whole business was laborious and deliberate. There was no such thing as a simultaneous submission. And then I waited for a response.

I didn't run out to the mail every day looking for an envelope I recognized, because I thought I'd be rejected by every place I submitted to. That wasn't what happened. To my surprise I received many personal responses from editors with their rejections, encouraging notes about my poetry, invitations to submit again, even some funny notes full of unexpected camaraderie. I even had an acceptance or two. In my letter I had introduced myself by saying these were my first submissions and that I had recently graduated from college. This was true. I had a few items on my résumé and hauled them out to make me seem less pathetic, but for the most part I presented myself for what I was— a rank beginner. Many of the editors who wrote back were sweet, happy even to make my acquaintance. But one editor, the poet, was downright offended that I had submitted my poems at all. I should add that in my submission letter I did not elicit advice or ask for a personal response. I thought it likely that all the editors would just reject me with the least amount of fuss and wasted time.

I was taken aback by receiving the handwritten letter from the poet. From her point of view I had submitted to a magazine above my rank. She thought that I was in need of a major correction and she was just the person to give it to me. I no longer have the letter. I wish I did. I kept it for years with other memorable documents, and it followed me up the coast to graduate school in Seattle, Washington, and across the country to my first job in Morgantown, West Virginia, and finally to East Lansing, Michigan. I'm not sure when I threw it away, when I decided I no longer needed to hold on to the actual letter for by then I had it by heart. I worried that if I died someone might come upon the most humiliating letter I have ever received. There was something shameful about the letter that I didn't want anyone to see. It made me feel like I had felt when my mother once slapped me across the face.

The poet pretended she was being kind to me, that it would be cruel for her to "encourage" me to continue writing poetry when I did it so poorly. Nothing good could possibly come from my writing and the sooner I confronted that *fact* and moved on the better I would be. Surely, she said, I did something better than the way I wrote poetry. She felt that by my submission of poems I presented a painful dilemma to *her*. The letter was all about *her*—her dilemma, how should she answer me, what response should she give? Years later when I read the letter I was struck that she presented *my* submission as a test of *her*. A young poet submits her poems to a literary magazine. Surely not a unique or earthshattering occurrence. The editor rejects them. Pretty simple. Editors have the power to accept and reject—that's what we know they will do. Even I in my infancy knew those were the choices. I did not expect editors to take me under their wing nor did I expect to be scolded for submitting my poems. My act triggered something deep and troubling in the poet. I knew it then but I didn't understand it, couldn't fathom what nerve I had struck.

I know it even more surely now. It would have been simpler to just reject me. Why take the time to compose a letter—a performance of kindness that masks ruthless aggression? Why did the poet feel it was her duty, her moral obligation to stop me from writing poems? She said that saying nothing struck her as worse than saying something that might dissuade me from continuing. In the course of one short letter she felt she needed to persuade me to abandon *my* illusions. I had no talent. I needed to see this about myself. She pointed me to a poem by Louise Glück that she felt would be instructive for me to read since it did successfully what my poem failed to do. I was well read in contemporary poetry for someone who had just graduated from college. I knew the Glück poem well. I owned Glück's second book of poems, *The House on The Marshland,* had dog-eared many of the poems. The poet brought my attention to "Pomegranate" and made me see my great mistake. Fool that I was, I had submitted a poem of my own called "Pomegranate." At the time I didn't have it in me to coolly compare Glück's magnificent poem and my paltry one. I took the poet's word for the disparity between the two. The poet might as well have waved Keats' "Ode to Autumn" in my face. I raised the flag of my surrender before I had begun. I wandered to another poem in the collection, "Love Poem," which the poet also directed my attention to, which begins "There is always something to be made of pain./Your mother knits." I'm embarrassed to admit how many hours I spent trying to figure out if the poet thought the pain she was inflicting upon me was something I needed, and that if I was worth anything, I would figure out what I could make of it. Or whether she was suggesting I take up knitting.

After she demolished my poem, she closed with perhaps the oddest part of all. She said that I was braver than her. And again I remember feeling that this encounter was personal to her in a way I couldn't fathom. I pictured the woman who wrote me as a close cousin to the headmistress of the girls high school I had attended. Lillian Thurman was the headmistress at Moravian Seminary for Girls. She lived on the campus with her mother. She was a thoroughly upright woman. She held herself so stiffly it was impossible to imagine she could bend even if she wanted to. She sat very tall in her hard-backed chair in the entrance every day before school started to check the length of our uniforms and whether we were wearing any forbidden jewelry. She made us kneel upon the floor and with a ruler she measured whether our skirt fell two inches below the knee, exactly. She wore cashmere sweaters, tweed skirts, and sensible shoes. Her gray hair was carefully coiffed off her face and she spoke with a southern accent. She was unmarried and upheld the rules without fail, showing no sympathy to any of the girls who were hers to manage, I say manage for surely she did not guide us. It seemed to me that Lillian Thurman hated us. Did she hate our youth, which she no longer possessed, that our lives stretched out before us and as yet no road chosen? Did she curse her fate that she was somehow, probably through no fault of her own, forced to be the headmistress of a herd of girls and have her mother in tow to boot, to lead a life she did not want? When I read the poet's letter, it was Lillian Thurman who I saw. Another woman who might have been a kind mentor but was not.

Some personal frustration crept into her letter to me. I wondered why she thought I was braver than her. It seemed to me that I had merely been foolish. Had she once been a young woman who harbored ambitions to write and did she not heed them? Did someone stop her as she was trying to stop me? Did she stop herself? What was her story? What was it that made her want to slap me down—the fact that I was doing what she wanted and yet I possessed so little talent compared to her?

I couldn't tally it all. All I knew was that the letter had succeeded in its mission. I pulled the shades in my bedroom and crawled into bed even though it was 3 o'clock on a Friday afternoon and I didn't get up again until Monday morning. I felt stricken, punched, a fool, an idiot, I spent the weekend lying there cycling through my hopes for myself and the reality that I was worthless and deluded. All my teachers who had encouraged me were wrong. The poet alone was correct in her assessment. I thought I'd run into some disappointments, rejections for sure; I just never figured another woman would want to take me down.

Of course at the reading I saw that my poet did not at all resemble my headmistress. At the time my poet had written me, she was a tender young woman, not middle-aged, unmarried, burdened with the care of her mother, and cooped up with a lot of unruly girls on an campus in the middle of nowhere. No, my poet was a beauty, a desired person, running in an elite crowd of writers and artists, the cream of the cream, and had through a story I didn't know and don't know risen to the role of poetry editor. I saw also that despite her youthful hesitancy to write herself, she had gone on to write and her work had found an audience and some measure of success.

In graduate school, having sufficiently made something out of my pain, I studied the modernist poet Louise Bogan, author of the ironic critique "Women," a poem that has troubled readers because it has been read as an uncharitable portrait of women. Yet one must never forget that Bogan was a woman who fully included herself in the collective portrait, that finally the poem's indictment turns upon its writer. Competition was fierce among women for coveted spots in journals, far fewer spots than we enjoy today. She tended to be a harsh judge of other women, as if she needed to distance herself from the crop of women poets, and an even fiercer critic of herself. She didn't think that she was in a battle with men, though she was; she thought women were her enemy. I've come to think that the crisis of kinship Bogan experienced has not entirely dissipated with the passage of time and my poet would not have felt the need to correct a young male writer who had submitted his poems before she deemed he was ready. She would not have written a personal letter to him informing him that he just didn't cut it and never would. That kind of presumption is admired in men, seen as necessary to get started, to go forth. The right stuff. She would have encouraged him, given him some hope.

At the time I did not stop to wonder at the differences in responses I received from editors based on their gender, but now I see that all the encouraging notes I received were written by men. My poet occupied a relatively unique position, a privileged position of being one of the few female editors at the time. Surely she was aware of her position and the power she could exercise. And in that way she was a bit like my headmistress. She did not have the power she wanted—the power to craft a poetry that suited her dreams for herself—but she did have some power, the power over her young female charges. She could help them or hurt them, she could make them kneel down before her.

Not long after my rejection, I received an issue of a small literary magazine called *Trellis*, edited by Maggie Anderson, with "Pomegranate," the very poem that had been seen as objectionable, in its pages. I had written the poem the winter of my sophomore year when Denise Levertov came to Wells College to teach for a few weeks in January. At the time Wells was on the four-one-four system in which students took one short but intensive course during the month of January. There were only about six of us enrolled in her class—we had to submit a portfolio to be selected. She was lodged in one of the college-owned cottages off campus, and for several afternoons a week we trudged through the snow to her door. We sat in her living room, arrayed around the fire, drinking tea she had made, sharing our poems, listening to her stories, following every turn of her beautiful head.

One afternoon in the middle of a discussion about line breaks, she sprung up from her chair and did a flip on the carpet to demonstrate how a poem has to leap from line to line, it has to have energy and verve, and, well, athleticism. We were stunned. No teacher had ever done a flip as a teaching lesson and no one has since. At the time she was no longer what you would call young. Her son was grown up. But she *was* young still, in mind and body, and was a woman of great zest. She was kind and she was tough, the two traits were not incompatible. She spoke her mind but without personal rancor. She told me I read my poems terribly, that racing through them at breakneck speed in a low, barely audible voice did a real disservice to them. My writing was better than that, she said, deserved better than I was giving it, and I should hold my head up and look straight ahead when I read. I did not feel attacked or humiliated. I felt released because what she said was true, anyone could see that what she said was true. It was also something I could change. She did not doom me to stewing in my own inferior juices for eternity.

At the end of our time together she asked me if she could have "Pomegranate." She had been asked to edit a section of poetry for a magazine—a section on new up and coming poets. Could she have my poem? As was perhaps indicative of my lack of confidence, I didn't quite believe her. I gave it to her at the end of January and never heard another word about it.

Several years had passed before *Trellis* arrived at my door. Maggie Anderson, the editor, didn't know where I was—I had moved many times since Wells. But here it was, "Pomegranate," the poem that Denise Levertov had found acceptable enough to publish and the poem the poet found woefully lacking any merit whatsoever. Who was right? Was I to choose? I tend to believe that the harshest assessment of my worth is the truest, but is it? I think it is safe to say that Louise Glück's "Pomegranate" is the far better poem, a poem that will stand the test of time. And mine will not. It is also true that I was submitting to a journal above my station and perhaps I should have known not to do that. But after all these years I do think she was trying to break me, to school me into silence. I've been rejected many times. Some of the rejections have stung, but that early one was a knockout punch—it was meant to land a blow and it did. I remember how it felt to be crushed. I wish I hadn't taken her criticism to heart, hadn't let it come inside me and take up residence there. I didn't have the tools to see that in part the quarrel she was having was with herself.

For years I thought the scene of rejection between the poet and me was static and unproductive. The poet was fixed in my mind as a terrifying figure and I was fixed, too, in my own insubstantiality. I see her now before me, leaning on the lectern at the front of the room, spent from her long reading, though, as ever, she does not see me. A crowd is moving toward her to congratulate her, as they should, for she has delivered her poems well. What I see now is that Glück was right. There is always something to be made of pain.

THE ART OF BEING BORN

Bride of Cows

rrive. Drive up the hill to the Virginia Center for the Creative Arts, keep a look out for the cows that have been reintroduced to the pastures. You don't spot any; wonder where they are. Park your car in the lot on the summit, walk along the little path to the front door. On the lobby wall, envelopes with keys and room assignments. The long corridor all the way to the end, to number 6, unlock the door and step in. Feel relief that nothing about the room has changed since your previous stay four years ago: the spotty beige carpet, the single bed without headboard, white cotton spread, the nightstand, lamp, and closet for the scant wardrobe of one person. You have crossed Michigan, down the slow side of Ohio, across Pennsylvania, into Maryland, briefly touching West Virginia and then finally passing into Virginia: your destination. You learned to count the states from your mother who woke you on car trips to announce entering a new state. This crossing over was important to her and now it is important to you.

ereft. The relief is short-lived. Tense and grief-weary— you are at odds with the sublime of the Blue Ridge Mountains. Feel your back buckle like a roof that's been exposed to the elements too long. It should bend, free as you suddenly are from all the tasks that have composed your life— no children to mother, no meals to prepare, no house to keep, no bills to pay, no sudden interruptions, no job to go to, no mother's funeral to orchestrate. Emerge from the room to bring your bags in from the car and immediately run into one of the Center's Fellows who wants to find out who you are: writer or painter. Writer, you say, mumbling something about exhaustion. Oh, she replies, disappointed. Walk the grounds in near dark; step behind a tree if some one approaches, avoid contact until you gain equilibrium. Notice now the shadowy presence of cows in the meadows that were empty on your last stay. Groups of them that form a greater whole of darkness. Look up on the top of the hill at the residence house, its beacon of lights lit like a cruise ship sailing dark waters, portholes aglow.

Change. You want to stand still yet there's a current of change flowing to your right, moving fast, sweeping everything with it. You have never felt that word so strongly as you do now. You are tilting to the right as the current moves downstream carrying your life with it. Just a month ago you were pruning the yellow rose in the side yard when your mother fell and her skull turned to mud. It was as if she slipped into a surging river and was swallowed. Mother, anchor: gone. One day you are a little girl holding an Easter basket standing on the front stoop with your mother and sisters and the next you're standing with your sisters tossing rose petals into the hole that holds your mother.

Dinner, the one meal eaten in common. Four years ago a balance of writers and painters waited hungrily for the door to the dining room to be opened. All the tables were filled and a line formed in front of the buffet. Now with the new roof being installed on the barn where the studios are housed, the fellows are a fraction of what they were, just two tables worth, and nearly all writers. It feels like you are a winter guest at a grand hotel closed for the season. You reside in rooms on separate wings, keeping your own time, rising and retiring when you wish, creating and observing your own rituals. There was more joy during your last stay. Now dinner conversation consists of the day's writing tallies, how many words written, how many erased, like a bed being made and unmade. This time it is like the end of something. Released into this bucolic paradise, the writers have carried with them the worm that flourishes, then ravages the rose.

Enter the web. Everywhere you go, a spider has spun an intricate net for the uninvited. You can't avoid them, you can't step round them; they hang from every carapace, every portal. Let the fat black spiders hanging in the middle of tender webs honor your face. Routinely an inchworm crawls on your shoulder; strands of web hang from your glasses. There is a time for writing and a time for wandering. This is your time to wander. Start at the bottom of the hill, at the far border where Route 29, a four-lane highway, washes by with fast cars. Pass over a cattle crossing on the narrow road that cuts up through meadows of uncut grass, knee-high, a pale wheat ending in burgundy tips the color of stewed plums, like a prairie transplanted to Virginia, along the wire fence that divides the cow pasture from the meadow and runs parallel to the train tracks. Cows in the fields lower their heads against the heads of others to protect themselves from the insects. When they look up at your approach, their ponderous heads are swarmed with black flies. Osage oranges dot this fence line, and as you walk, oranges fall, not singly but simultaneously, with solid thumps, and then roll until they come to rest, undamaged, ripe and riddled with black veins like drawings of the brain. Walk up the hill, the muscles in the back of your legs tightening, your back aching to meet the rise. Something exhilarates you—to be out in broad daylight, in the open, at noon. The distant traffic on Route 29 buzzes faintly; a train approaches on the nearby tracks and passes. A door somewhere (everywhere) opens and closes.

Frail and decrepit, the fence fails to keep the cows in the pasture. Three stand in the middle of the drive as you swing your car out of the parking lot and over the cattle guard and down the hill to post a letter. A tall black calf turns to face the vehicle, leaning awkwardly into the road, and you brake. Until this visit you thought of cows in the uniform images of a children's story book: the pure black Angus, the black-and-white Holstein. But these three don't fit neatly together: a tall, stocky blonde stands next to a flop-eared, humpbacked, mouse-colored something, next to the all-black. You think the cows will give way to the car and move to the side of the road. Surely they are intimidated. They are not. You are helpless before them. Back up to the top of the crest, turn around, and drive to the office to inform the secretary, as you have been instructed, that three cows are loose though not on the run. Forget your errand.

Garage sale: *Baby shoes. Never used.* At dinner another resident claims Hemingway wrote the words in a competition for the best shortest story. It's a good story, the story that it's his story, though he didn't go to garage sales. All night trying to write one. Up come nine words: "When I swim the sidestroke, I become my mother." Hemingway did say, "All stories, if continued far enough, end in death."

Home. Thinking of it, getting calls, nothing good. You stand on the porch and look over the fields like water in the failing light and mountains bruised purple. Lights start and stop on the road: cows caught in the headlights. And then in a stutter of footwork, the cows cross to the other side. You write a poem:

> There is a knock on my windowpane
> which cracks and my mother rises
> from the cool sap of the earth.
> Come in I say. I know
> you want to lie down next to me,
> let your veil fall and drift
> sallow about my face.
> I ask her to tell me how long
> she has been dead.
> Not long, she says.

I, I, you say. How tiring being an "I." You lie awake at night, unsteady in a place where everything has been arranged for the ease of the "I." Truths you face: distaste for being human, the ways humans move through the world, thinking we should get our way, we should put our stamp on things. The herding instinct, you wish you had it.

Joy. Winding your way down to the lower meadow and finding the cows lying there where the road curves sharp right and a few oaks make a noontide shade. All sizes and colors down under the trees where the field is yellow. A few others, motley and broken off from the group, stand in the road or on its lip doing absolutely nothing. The very largest are a color hard to name—not white and not gray, a color like coffee whitened with cream and gone cold.

K evin, a writer of crime novels, is disturbed by your intimacy with the cows. He stops you on the path because you are looking at the juvenile bulls. "You're not supposed to stare at the bulls," he says in a scold. "You'll rile them up." He throws this back over his muscled shoulder as he hurries along to his labors. The bulls bend their heads to the grass like a Baroque oil of the shepherds' adoration.

Later at dinner, feeling his words did not impress you, Kevin tells a cautionary tale: "An elderly couple made the mistake of making a pet of the young beef bull they were raising. Like the bulls you were staring at this morning." He lifts his eyes from the plate to see the effect upon you. Your eyes are veiled. The last thing you want is to turn a cow into a pet. Cutting his broccoli into small pieces, he continues. "When he got to be a yearling and started feeling manly, he attacked the husband one day when he came inside the feeding pen. He got the man down and butted and trampled him to death. When the wife went into the pen to help, she, too, was killed." You think of your mother's silent fall, the shock of it, but say nothing.

L ast things found in your mother's room: 3 pairs of glasses, all bi-focal, large framed, out of style, and dirty, one bar of soap—round, small, waxy, colorless, not white, not cream, not yellow, shocking pink plastic hair brush, black bristles clogged with grey hair, lipstick, green metallic case, body powder puff and case called Heaven Sent, pale yellow shower cap hanging on the shower knob, a blue mohair coat for a doll, empty medicine bottles thrown in the trash with a torn up letter from twenty years ago written from a lost daughter, empty shoe boxes, Blue Grass toilet water, pictures fallen off the walls, never rehung, a broken toilet seat, 2 nightgowns, Vanity Fair make, one pink, one blue, both stained.

M easuring time, walking up and down the road. Each time you run into the cows, count an impasse: impasse number 1, impasse number 2, and so on. Walking for the exercise, you tell others, and in the beginning it was true. But now you're walking to see the cows. You're walking for the impasse

Night. Near the oaks at the bottom of the drive, cows down in the tall pale grass. A dream. Sitting in a wooden chair blunt and small, a chair from grade school, you are a bride in a long-sleeved black gown with a plastic veil that blots out your view. A great bouquet of red roses spills their juice onto your lap. The black veil a blindfold, and you a prisoner.

Odd that tonight your watch should stop at exactly 6:00, the hour when your father insisted dinner be served upon his return from work, the hour your mother miserably struggled to present the meal, the hour when your parents were presumably to come together in some kind of domestic harmony, but merely brought their marital stiffening to the table. On this night the dead won't stay in their pasture.

Pulled to a place where nothing much happens. Day after day. Restless, waiting to break through the impasse. Two hawks hang in the blue sky. At first they seem to need no effort, their wings extended and still, tilting first to the right, and then to the left, as the wind currents twist them about. Then, after long minutes, they flap their wings, circle, and hang again. The appearance of effortlessness is sham. It takes energy pulled from the air to keep the hawks aloft, presiding over the field below. They wait to see what the tractor disturbs with its mowing, to see what mouse may be turned out of its shelter that they might strike and kill. The hawks and you keep at your vigilance, keep in a posture of readiness, necks slightly bent, eyes focused down and out, backs taut, hearts pumping as fast as the train rushing under the bridge. You think if you concentrate hard enough . . .

Quarter to eight in the morning, walk down the road through the lower pasture. On the right side a quintet of cows, gathered by Lorca's sculpture, a block of brown-veined alabaster. The cows like the patch of grass the gardener mows round this giant eye that glares from the prairie. Frisking with one another, rubbing and butting heads, pushing together into the road and down the shoulder into the fence. Some are hurrying over from the field across the road. The is the first time you have seen a cow rush anywhere. Near the end of the field, needing to cross the road, they stand and moo. They *bellow* like a bugle announcing the arrival of a magnificent guest.

Remembering the first shower you took after your mother died. "This is the first shower since she died," you announced though no one else was in the bathroom. Then there was the first meal, the first laughter, but not the first tears because then you could not cry. Dry-eyed is what you were—nothing brought you to tears, not a twisted ankle or a busted nose, not the sight of an elderly woman reaching for a wall to brace herself—until coming here and now they're coming, the tears. Tears run into your ears, your mouth, down your neck into the crease between your breasts.

Shoo, Lorca says to the cows worshipping at her sculpture. They are dark blocks of marble gathered about it and so numerous that they spread across the road. The cows rub up against her sculpture—you worry they will knock it over. She claps her hands and shoos them again, over and over till they break up and float away, in a tempo like a slow heartbeat. You walk in the spaces between them into the remaining light.

Tango. Impasse number 55. Will the cows turn their great shoulders and shamble away upon your approach? Will you walk through the cows, dive in head first? No guts, no glory. You clap your hands and shoo them like Lorca. Nothing happens. Cows look at you as if they know you. You dip and glide through them, very close. You expect mud breath, pasture parsley and tongue slatherings. You expect to feel their flanks mottled with welts and cuts. Their breath is hot, exhalations of gusts of steam that hang in the air sweetly. And though a thousand flies land on their skin a day, you find no open sores.

Unseen through the grasses on the curve of the hill, for both sides of the meadow rise up around you to provide cover, as if cut out of all the family photographs.

Vexing. An apple you can't be fond of, spongy like moss, packed in your lunch pail. An apple packed especially for you. You should eat it, not good to waste food. Nibble at the edges. Not much progress, hardly one slope is dented, and back into your pail. Alone on the path to the cows, open your pail, and take out the apple. One of the largest cows, beige, lies near the fence. Throw the apple softly near her, but not too near, not to startle her. Prone, she looks at the apple, then struggles to her great bony knees and rises up, like an ancient curtain that jerks away to reveal the stage. A few steps to the apple, she noses it, pushes it a foot away and snatches it whole into her mouth. She crunches down once and swallows. Remembering your mother turning an apple in her hands, deciding where to start, where to puncture the lustrous globe.

Walk down the drive in your blue rain slicker and frighten one of the calves, lost in a reverie of chewing. It bolts from the fence, scampers skittishly fifty yards away and abruptly stops to look at you. You look back. You reach out your hand as if to touch. It resumes chewing.

Xout the last day on the calendar. Pack up the contents of number 6 and load your car. Walk down the tree-shrouded road lit only by the full moon and stars, through numberless cows towards a patch of light as if a curtain were parting. Feel them turn towards you, grazing your sides. You smell them—a smell like warm mud. Walk to the middle of the bridge that crosses above the tracks, stop dead over them, and face eastward from whence the Crescent will be coming at 10:53. See its light—a burning white powdery kind of light—before you see the body of the train, before you hear it. It is fast then, coming towards you, parting the fields in two, both sides dark. A humid gust on your face, and then you raise your arm and hold it outstretched, unsure if anyone conducting can see you in the dark above, in the middle of the bridge. When the Crescent rushes under, the whistle blows, and before you can count to three, it has passed under and long gone, a bullet of light.

Y ears thus, and more years, swimming through this grass to a noon shade, to float in its dark pool.

Z ion, in the morning, before anyone stirs, leave it. Lock number 6, put the key back in the envelope, place it in the mailbox. Back out the front door, along the little path to the parking lot high above the front pasture. Swing out of the lot, over the cattle guard and down the hill, past Lorca's sculpture, stopping to dump a bag of apples under the trees in the curve of the road where the cows will gather come noon. Turn to the right onto Route 29, join the fast traffic washing by.

The Making of Mothers: Portraits

The Laugh of Medusa

This one's a mother who with each passing year becomes more selfless. This is a mother who is dropping everything of hers to do her daughter's bidding. At her daughter's bidding, this is a mother who is passing away into selflessness, more and more, more and more she is dropping everything that is hers, to buy groceries, to take her daughter clothes shopping, to keep her cupboards appealing.

This is a mother who more and more is asking if her daughter needs anything. Care and worry, care and worry, the giver, the care giver, the wart, the worry wart. Always giving, never taking. To her daughter this is a mother who is becoming old, tired, and weary. This is one who is napping in the back seat of cars, dozing in movies. This is a mother who can't stay awake.

But sometimes when she is not making her cupboards appealing, when she isn't dropping everything that is hers, she begins laughing and the laugh that is coming out of her gets louder and louder and she can't stop the laugh and the laugh becomes all there is coming out of her, and the daughter struggles to understand her mother's laugh, she struggles to understand what is coming out of her selfless mother, the one who is always asking her what she needs. She wants the mother to control herself because the laughing is getting louder and louder until the mother is disappearing inside the laugh and the daughter wants the laugh to stop.

The White Goddess

This is a mother who thinks she should be found in the kitchen morning, noon, and night. This is one who thinks she should be an appliance, a permanent fixture like a microwave, ready to spring into use when her hungry daughter wanders into the kitchen. She thinks she shouldn't look like an appliance, all hard pnd cold and made of steel, but she should be *like* an appliance with buttons that her daughter can push. On/Off. On/Off. This is a mother who thinks she should be standing in the kitchen, ready and waiting, in a white apron. This is a mother who thinks she should wear pearls when she is cooking. A theme of white. This is a mother who thinks these white things but gets the family's dinner from a drive-thru. This is a mother who can't stand in the kitchen because she is standing in a bank, counting other people's money. This is a mother who fingers the dollar bills of strangers and thinks about where she is supposed to be so that her daughter could find her morning, noon, and night, but she never is. This is a mother who thinks about snow.

The Mother Knot

This is a mother who is always furious with her daughter, furious because her daughter is not liking pink. This one is a mother who won't accept that her daughter is not liking pink and decorates her room in pink. Not a dash of pink, here and there, not just an accent of pink, a swirling pattern of pink roses on a bedspread, or a pink bud vase. No. Every inch of wood is lacquered the pinkest of pink. Pink hangers and pink liners for pink drawers, a pink shoe case hanging from a pink closet door, pink light switches and pink doorknobs, a pink mirror and pink light bulbs to bathe her daughter in an everlasting pink glow. Even the stars outside the window seem pink. This is a mother who wonders where her daughter goes when she is avoiding her room. Her daughter is outside in the green as much as possible, down the alley, furrowed in weeds, in the fields, by the river, hanging from trees. Her mother is furious. This is a mother who is pushing her daughter to be liking what her mother is liking, to be being who her mother is being. The more she pushes, calling her daughter hers, the more the daughter is pulling away from the mother. The more the daughter is pulling away from the mother, the more the mother is feeling furious, so furious that she is on the verge of exploding, going up in a puff of smoke.

The Elementary Structures of Kinship

The rhythm of the mother's chopping onions hurts her daughter's soul. Chop. Chop. Chop. Pause.

    Hurt.

The top of this mother's lip curls before the difficulty of the onion. What is the difficulty of this onion, the daughter thinks, and why are her eyes tearing up? Is it from the milky sap of the onion or the skin of the mother? Chop. Chop. Chop. Pause.

Hurt.

The mother looks up from her onion and wipes her eyes. The daughter, too, has tears and thinks—are my mother's tears caused by the onion or has she read my mind? Does my mother know that she irritates my soul?

The mother holds out the knife to her daughter: "Will you chop awhile? My eyes," she says.

The daughter takes the knife silently from her mother and begins chopping. Chop. Chop. Chop. Pause.

Hurt.

The Mother Who Can't Finish Her Sentences

This is a mother who can't finish her sentences and wishes she could but she is perpetually stranded in the middle of a blue-veined thought, one flash propels her forward into the morning to the cries echoing from inside the open bedroom door and another flash turns her back in a circle to midnight and the porch where her own mother once called her to come home, no stroke sees her safely to shore to the end of the white corridor of time, no stroke straightens out the serpentine course of rescues and mistakes, the family all tucked tightly into their respective beds, no matter how hard this mother presses her temples her thoughts loop from cry to call a catalogue of loss, from bed to bed, moment to moment in a score of moments as the wind is always moving, touching but never resting, each air draft inseparable pushing along in an upward current into a sky that loves her.

Love Song: The Reproduction of Mothering (1)

This is a mother who still holds her daughter's hand when they're walking down the street. Her daughter is eighteen years old. This is a mother who wants her daughter to look and act and be just like her. This is a daughter who does not resist what her mother wants. As the years pass, this is a daughter who is becoming her mother. This is a mother who is always receding into the background. This is a mother who is always refilling platters, emptying trash, washing dishes. This is a daughter who with each passing year is receding into the background, watching her brother from the wings doing his tricks, clapping along with her mother and others. This is a mother who wears little Sunday school white gloves to bed to keep her hands innocent. This is a daughter who in time will too.

Portrait of the Artist: The Sorrow Eater

This is a mother who, as she is walking home from work after a long day, eats the sorrow that is seeping out of the windows of parked cars, leaking out of the averted eyes of the passersby, oozing from the cracks of the sidewalk. This is a mother who is getting fat with the world's sorrow. This is a mother to whom stories snake out of the dense ivy that would make you weep if you could hear them. This is a mother who doesn't turn away from what makes her weep—the story of the child who sat on her front stoop waiting for her parents to come home until the cement froze over with ice; the story of the child who disappeared with the bottle of milk her mother sent her to fetch; the story of the mother who lost her daughter when the ice broke on the river her daughter was skating. This is a mother who is a poet, though no one knows it, not even the mother.

Love Song: The Reproduction of Mothering (2)

This is a mother who when she was a girl was afraid of the mother. The mother turned down the sheets of her bed through soft ferns of moonlight while the father turned the pages of newspaper under bright lamp light. As a girl she heard the mother breathing through the open window and she was afraid. The mother brushed the girl's hair and polished her shoes. She learned how to cook the meals the girl liked. Yet each night when the mother filled the tub with hot clean water and called the girl to come home with *It's time and the water is running*, the girl stepped back through the trees.

Now the girl has become a mother herself. There is no part of her now that is not a mother. There was a person before she became a mother. She writes about that person, visits photographs in which she is depicted. She sees the fear in her face like a trapped animal. But now as a mother she steps out of the trees and feels exposed. She calls her daughter to come home, *It's time and the water is running*, and she is afraid her daughter won't come.

The Art of Being Born

In what I hoped would be our final appointment with the midwife, she guessed that you weighed eight pounds, four ounces, and that you would come soon.

That morning I woke up late, having spent the night beached on the couch in the living room, memorizing the distinguishing signs of every rash chronicled in Dr. Spock's baby book, until nodding off around six. The book lay open to cradle cap, flaking patches of skin on top of a newborn's head that might be "cracked, greasy, or even weeping."

It was ten days past the date when you were supposed to arrive, and I was too uncomfortable, too wrung out with anxiety, to sleep. Early in pregnancy women can forget they are pregnant for an hour or two, a day perhaps. They can walk the fields at their usual pace, bend down and lift laundry baskets easily. They can hop, skip, jump, and run after a bus pulling away from the curb. In the last trimester every second is colored with the knowledge that you have something living inside you and it's growing—it's pushing against your being. When you turn on your side, you are turning for two. Nothing about me remained as it was. In the last weeks, after an hour or so of tossing in bed each night, I'd shuffle out to the couch so that your father might sleep undisturbed. In the mornings I'd lumber into the shower, brace my arms against the walls, stand under the spray, letting the water rain down on my face and stream over my breasts and enormous stomach, and I would cry.

But this morning I waddled to the bedroom and sagged in the doorway. Your father took one look at my forlorn figure and said, "Come on, let's get out of here."

We walked, taking our way slowly down 22nd Street to Ravenna Park, and then inside the park to its old-growth ravine. As we entered the muddy trail down to Ravenna Creek, Richard took my hand in his to brace me for our descent. Freshwater springs welled from the tall walls of sedimented rock and flowed down into the stream. We mimicked the first untroubled humans, trudging on the path that looped through the waterlogged bottoms, Richard slowing his pace, me trying to move myself forward. At the end of the mile loop we huffed up from the ravine and emerged by the tennis courts, where we rested a bit, sitting on a bench beneath a bracelet of blooming cherry trees, the branches dipping down around us to offer their gifts.

It was nearly noon, and I lay on my side on the bench and put my head in Richard's lap. We spoke of our anticipation, and wondered how much longer we would wait for you, our first child. I had been steadfastly uninterested in having children. Nothing moved me from my refusal—not holding a newborn in my arms, not the transformative tales of motherhood. I was too wrapped up in the trouble of being a daughter waiting for her mother's love that would never come, and I was surprised when I was seized by a great longing for a child. At that moment we weren't anxious. How could we be anxious, sitting on the warm bench in the sun, the world alive and green, and the branches of the cherry trees framing our hopes?

I'm telling you this because no event is more momentous than birth. Every girl wants to know about her beginning and asks, *Where did I come from?* Many children are answered with a birth story that speaks to the child of who she is and will be, a story that sets her life in motion on a particular path. Mothers tell this story to the child again and again, like a favorite fairytale, as she rests her head on her pillow at night, listening devoutly, mulling deeply, drifting down on her way to peaceful sleep.

But sometimes the stories of origin are troubled, riven with complexity and unanswered questions that bespeak a cloudy future.

My parents never spoke of the circumstances surrounding my birth, and I am in possession of only a few meager facts.

> *I was born on February 26 in the stark of winter.*
> *No baby pictures were taken.*
> *No baby book, where the important milestones are recorded, exists.*
> *I was installed in a wood-paneled room down a long corridor at the back of the house.*

My mother's silence on the subject of my birth led me to believe that the day, the event, my entrance onto the stage of her life, was complicated by emotions I didn't understand and would never understand. I came to think, perhaps irrationally, my birth was a mistake, and that was why all the memorializing forms were blank. Instead of caressing the event in memory, my mother entered a state of amnesia from which she never awoke.

On the bus ride to school, while some of my girlfriends were choosing names for their future children, I'd make up stories of my birth, like a character in search of a play. The births I imagined took place out of doors, as if I were a wild animal:

In fields
In meadows
In mountains
In a valley
In the woods
In a ravine
Beside a stream

In these stories my mother and I were always alone, mother and daughter, the essential couple.

Here is one story I made up, picturing it more than finding the words:

> On a Sunday morning in September, my mother drove out of town, deep into the country of farms and pastures and ponds, until she reached an apple orchard. The trees stood under an open sky, rugged and strong on a rough incline. My mother passed among them, pulling red globes from the branches and putting them gently in her bag, while other apples, too ripe to wait for her hand, dropped thudding to the ground. She made a bed below the boughs, sank down among the fallen fruit, and I was born.

This story is preposterous on many levels. I wasn't born in September. I never knew my mother to pick fruit, and certainly the apples we ate were all store-bought. You can tell I didn't know the first thing about birthing. My mother giving birth beneath a tree, as if she were a doe and I her fawn, is a fairytale. My mother never lay in the grass. We never had a picnic, even at a table. Yet despite its utter lack of veracity, this was one of my birth stories.

I always used to think, when I pondered my missing birth story, that I was the wounded party. It never occurred to me that I wasn't the only one who had been deprived of a birth story one would want to share. It never occurred to me that there were no baby pictures because my mother was denied access to me in the first weeks. In her proper social circle, birth wasn't talked about. Women didn't share the gritty details, the bloody show. A doctor and medical staff kept women medicated and deadened to the actuality of birth. Perhaps my mother never spoke of my birth because she didn't know the details. In some ways, she wasn't present for my birth—she was the vessel that carried me. She was knocked out—there's no other way of putting it. She saw me only through the nursery window, too sedated to hold me. And then she went home without me. My mother had little say in choosing her experience and little to say about it. And she never talked about what had been denied her.

After my mother's death, my father discovered a cache of photographs she had stashed away. All the photos were a revelation; just their existence required me to rethink my portrait of my mother. But one photo stood out: it was a baby picture of me. No one is holding me, neither my mother nor my father. I'm lying awake on my mother's bed, the one place where I most longed to be as a child. In this photograph I seem to be looking up at the person taking the photo. There is a shadow, my mother's, pointing the camera. The bedspread is white, and the blankets I'm swaddled in are white. I look small and dwarfed among the snowy folds. I'm holding my hands up in a defensive position, and my hands are clenched. I can hardly say what I felt looking at this picture after having spent the bulk of my life believing no pictures of me as a baby existed. And here I was, at long last, on my mother's bed. It's just a little square photo, so small it could easily have disappeared and never been recovered. But it has; it is a fact, and like other facts, it complicates everything.

After our afternoon appointment with Patricia, our midwife, we drove home across the floating bridge, its latched-together segments like a construction toy, with a rough thump after each piece. We ate dinner and watched the Sonics playoff game on our tiny black-and-white TV, which Richard set up on a bench in front of the couch. Around halftime I started having contractions. Just in case this was the real thing, I packed my suede blue overnight bag and put it by the door. In it, along with a copy of our birth plan, clothes for you and clothes for me and whatnot, was my hospital reading material, Nietzsche and Schopenhauer, which I needed to get a grasp of for my upcoming exams. (You are shaking your head and laughing—I obviously knew nothing about labor or hospital stays.) Unlike my mother, who had no training and no birth partner, we had prepared in a class offered by the midwife's clinic that included drafting a birth plan. Yes, we had a plan. We paid scant attention to the physical exercises but spent an inordinate amount of time figuring out what music we wanted to hear during labor, as if it were a dance party requiring a playlist. The birth plan called for a teddy bear—a focal point to concentrate on during contractions—a mat to lie on, and a baby bag full of clothes and blankets for you. All of this was in the bag too.

When it started looking bad for the Sonics, Richard hauled the birthing assemblage to our car, filled with boxes of books we had neglected to clear out. The time between contractions was shortening, and they were intensifying, rapidly and uncomfortably so. It seemed like real labor, what we had been waiting for, not a false alarm, not the practice Braxton Hicks contractions. We called Patricia and were told to come on in. Back into our little Civic we went, packed now as if we were heading on safari.

The ride, our second over the bridge in not many hours, was excruciating. The rhythmic bounce of the car as it passed over each seam shot pains through my back. Richard tried to listen to the basketball game through my groans. Back to the parking lot that five hours ago seemed like optimistic heaven, only now I could barely lift myself out of the car or walk across the lot. If I didn't move, I speculated, the contractions might not be so bad, or might not come at all.

Inside the maternity ward Patricia measured my cervix, which was just as it had been earlier in the day. She wasn't certain I was in real labor. Unless she declared labor, I couldn't be admitted to the hospital, couldn't be assigned my own room. I was instructed to walk up and down the back stairwells to stimulate labor. The optimism of the morning under the cherries had vanished.

At eleven o'clock she measured me once again. Slight progress, but not enough to declare active labor. Patricia sent us off wandering once again. Midnight came, and still I hadn't been formally admitted. We climbed a few stairs, only to have me fall against the cement wall and slump to the steps when a contraction seized me.

You should know that contractions operate in stages like a thunderstorm. They rumble toward you from far off, tremors building at a distance, until they arrive dead center. When they reach full strength, every inch of your body is taken captive by the seizure, and there's nothing you can do but give in to its superior power. And then, when you have been wrung out, the storm lets you go and rumbles off until the next tremor begins.

When a contraction lifted, Richard hauled me to my feet, and we once again climbed the stairs. Up and down we went, stopping and starting, until we exited the stairwell and staggered by the nurse's station like beggars searching for a handout.

"Couldn't someone do something? Give me something to move the labor along or ease the pain?"

"No," replied the nurse at the station, referring me brusquely to my birth plan, which was pinned on her clipboard. The plan firmly stated my opposition to drugs. I wanted a natural birth, to be awake and alert, to feel everything. "What you are going through is perfectly normal," the nurse said. "Not an emergency."

I screamed—I'm sure I screamed—"But I didn't know what labor was when I wrote the plan! Give me something, *please.*" She offered me ice chips. Richard rubbed my back. I cried.

I thought I was going to die, and that you would never live through this torture. How could something so painful result in you? How could babies survive the turmoil of birth, the violence of it? Because make no mistake, labor is violent: it squeezes the air out of you. In the moments between contractions, when pain waited in the wings, I thought about women who had given birth before me, women who were at this very instant giving birth in hospitals, in fields, in apartments, in elevators and makeshift infirmaries, women of all colors, sizes, shapes, who spoke languages I couldn't understand and ate food I had never tasted. We were united by this scorching labor.

At half past midnight Patricia rechecked me. I had progressed and was officially declared in labor and admitted to the hospital. I was going to have you after all. Finally we moved to the birthing room we had toured nearly nine months ago, decorated like a bedroom, with cheery pictures on the walls, rocking chairs, and a flower-patterned quilt. The walls were mauve with a burgundy border—rich and warm. Unfortunately, by this time labor was so advanced that I was barely conscious of the decor that had been so important to me in the planning stages. I lay down in the quilt-covered bed, but had even more difficulty getting through the pain. I tensed up, gripped Richard. I forgot about the quick shallow puffs of breath I had practiced in class. I cried and looked to Richard, who was the only person in the room, for Patricia was busy with another mother-to-be. I refused to let him go, even to bring our birthing accoutrements in from the car. I was long past teddy bears and playlists. I looked into his face during the contractions as he dutifully chanted, "Breathe, breathe, breathe."

When a contraction was done with me, I drifted out of consciousness, far away, leaving behind a black and frightening sky. Spent, and traveling out of the body, I returned to the apple orchard of my earlier birth fantasy. Now the trees were in blossom, in sunlight, under a pale blue heaven, and my friend Elizabeth, whose daughter Emma was born a year before, stood beneath them. Between contractions I went to this place where they waited and seemed to be welcoming me. Emma was perched on her mother's hip, stiff legs supported by her mother's cradled arm, while the canopy of branches crowned Emma's head. Her mother grasped an apple, pulling it down as her daughter pushed on her stomach to reach the blossoms waiting above.

Our midwife returned and saw how shaken and pale Richard was. He looked like he was going to faint. He alone had been my companion in labor; it was his face I looked at when trying to focus through the contractions, his hands I gripped, his voice trying to talk me through the pain, and it was his frame upon which I collapsed. There was no one else in the hours between arrival and admittance.

"Go down to the cafeteria," Patricia said. "Get some coffee, something to eat. It's going to be a while before the next stage." I let go of his hand that I had been holding onto like a life raft in a pulsing storm.

When Richard came back to the room I was in transition, the period between the first stage of labor and the last, when you push the baby out. I had been drifting in and out of consciousness when suddenly I got up, went to the bathroom, and threw up. The mucus plug that blocks the opening of the cervix was expelled and my water broke. It was as if a small balloon had burst, and out came the water in one big gush. And then I had to push. There was no stopping, no slowing the need to push, a push that originated somewhere far behind me, a great epic push and I no more than its instrument.

Now husband, midwife, and nurse huddled about the fetal monitor, which had started to register distress. Something was wrong—I could hear it in their voices, in the low tones, though I couldn't understand what they said. I was concentrating on pushing. I was told I had to get out of my bed and lie on a gurney that rolled in. Away I went, wheeling toward an operating room. Patricia was trying to slow down my pushing—there was talk of a C-section, getting you out quickly, calling a surgeon. But I couldn't stop pushing, and you crowned. Richard said he could see your head. I had never heard such excitement in his voice. Out you rushed with the umbilical cord lassoed around your neck. That's what was causing the distress. Each time I pushed, the cord tightened around your neck, cutting off oxygen and blood. But what could have been dire was not. Patricia was able to unloop the cord, and all was well. It was 4:19 a.m. on April 18, and you weighed eight pounds, four ounces. They wiped you off, wrapped you in a blanket, and put you in my arms.

A new story was born, one I am passing onto you. If you have reason to look back in puzzlement, wondering how you came into the world, remember I know the story of your birth—the art of being born—by heart.

How to Leave a Room

When you leave a room, my mother taught me, leave no trace behind. She trained me to be in a room without making it dirty.

And yet, to my confusion, she wore lipstick, applied in a thick style that changed little from year to year, a signature of sorts. In the bathroom she had her own sink, mirror, and cabinet. Out of the top drawer of the vanity she'd pull her single tube of lipstick—Revlon's Mercy, a buoyant shade of red, a bit shrill. Leaning close to the mirror, she puckered her lips and applied her Mercy, careful to stay inside the lines. At the end of the application, she'd brusquely rip a tissue from a nearby box and blot. And there would be the telltale red imprint of a kiss.

Now I have my own favored lipstick, a shade called Black Honey, more stain than matte rouge, and it is one of the mysteries about me my daughter cannot unravel. She belongs to a different generation, one addicted to all manner of exotic lubrication for the lips, carried in the pocket of the jeans, flavored in mango, and applied copiously. But she resists lipstick as cosmetic. The motto is Pierce, Don't Paint, spoken with a lisp on studded tongues.

Not long ago I overheard my daughter extolling the virtues of the natural look to her friend. They disapproved of my lips of dark honey.

"My mother wears lipstick to rake leaves," my daughter said, smacking her gum. "She puts lipstick on to take out the trash. To go swimming. She's got to have it on to open presents on Christmas morning."

"I don't get it," her friend chimed in. "Who is she putting lipstick on *for*?" Her pierced eyebrows, no doubt, were raised in bafflement.

"She doesn't *need* lipstick," concluded my daughter. I suppose she meant that my face was not such a diminished thing as to require the uplift. The words were solemnly spoken, without a trace of irony, as if she had settled a world conflict.

Does anyone need lipstick? It will not shelter me in a windstorm, nor feed me when I'm hungry. It can't perform miracles. Looked at from a certain angle, it can be dispensed with, thrown in the trash.

The Black Honey is, I admit, too noir for the norms of my professional class, which prefers the illusion of transparency. The attention drawn to my mouth is a little nervous. But then I am a little nervous, lurking about in alleys in the rain. Could I not dispense with this excess and simplify my life, or at least my face?

Why, then, do I wear it? I cannot justify it by naming any purpose but pleasure. I wear lipstick as some women wear high heels—defiantly. It's a mark I leave behind on cheeks, on glasses, on pillowcases, on memory. It throws people off. Lipstick is my excess, a mark of twisted allegiance to my mother.

After my mother died, I sorted through the mountains of details she left behind. In the vanity I found her familiar tube of red, worn down to the nub. I was overcome with a desire to smear my lips with her color, to be enamored with all her accoutrements and accessories. But there was no color left to apply.

Imagine going through your mother's purse and finding a tissue on which she had blotted her lips, leaving a perfect imprint. I don't know what you would do, but I would hold onto that tissue to eternity.

Pose

In my early reading, when I was introduced to some of the most important books of my life, I encountered the work in editions that did not include a photo of the writer. I read leather-bound editions of Charles Dickens, George Eliot, and Thomas Hardy that my mother had been given by her English ancestors, books housed in a case with glass doors in the living room. Propped up on a stack of pillows during a bad bout with chicken pox in the ninth grade, I read prized copies of *Jane Eyre* and *Wuthering Heights*, large hardbound volumes with forest-green bindings and gothic woodcuts of the moors and haunted landscapes of Brontë country by Fritz Eichenberg. His portrait of Heathcliff leaning against a tree with eyes cast heavenward in wrathful agony has always been my portrait of Heathcliff, and when I think of the girls that Jane joined at Lowood School, I see before me a woodcut of girls bent solemnly in two perfect columns, walking with eyes cast downward as if marching to a sentence of death. But I couldn't have told you what the writers looked like, nor did I desire their image. Their stories were more than enough. I often wondered if reading *Jane Eyre* and *Wuthering Heights* in the sickbed looking out on a landscape of swirling snow was when I began thinking I might be a writer, that I saw myself as someone who didn't want to be consoled. I wanted to burn.

It wasn't until much later, in college, that I began to match images of writers to their words. Over the years of my reading life I have glanced at hundreds of authors' images in books or dust jackets, and I've absorbed them without considering them a special species of portraiture. But nowadays a writer's identity is constructed through the image of the "author's photograph." It's impossible to read *Mrs. Dalloway* without the iconic image of Virginia Woolf in the forefront of one's mind. Barnes & Noble got her likeness silkscreened onto a million canvas bags, and the National Portrait Gallery in London sells thousands of Woolf postcards a month. Her image is plastered on mugs and T-shirts and all manner of merchandise.

In preparation for the publication of my first book, I was asked to produce my own author's photograph. I was such a rube to the world of literary publicity that I didn't realize I should have such a photo taken, and instead pulled out my albums and began the search for a suitable photo. I soon discovered that as an adult I took a better picture when in the presence of others. If I was the sole subject of the photograph, unease pulled my face into a tight, unhappy mask. I did not look like a woman happy to be the subject of attention. The writer, that mythic creature who has mastered shutting down disturbance and self-doubt, was nowhere to be found in my photos. My writer self was inextricably bound to all the other selves I embodied—mother, wife, teacher, friend.

It's one thing to be the subject of a photograph without knowing it. Someone snaps your photo while you're blessedly ignorant of the shot. It's another thing to consent and participate in the photograph, to know you are the primary subject posing in front of the lens. All my training, all the lessons I had learned about my proper insignificance conspired against seeing myself as a suitable subject of a photographic portrait. Coming from a family of insurance salesmen, dentists, and pump inventors, it didn't seem possible that I could be a writer even though I was. I have always thought of myself as a secondary subject, a minor character on stage, someone who assisted but was not the focus. In theater I imagined myself as the maid, carrying in platters of food, answering the phone, opening the door and taking a bow in a group after the main players took their solo bows. I didn't imagine myself as the one who would make a grand entrance and then hold forth in a long monologue or sing a solo.

A photo in which I share the spotlight with others is not what my publisher meant by an author's photograph, no matter how well it might represent something true about me. I learned this the hard way, after I sent a few photos that were rejected as being too candid and informal. What was wanted was a photo with me as the solitary subject, looking like a writer. What does it mean, I asked, to look like a writer? Could I see my writer-self while writing and try to copy what I observed? In one photo I sent I was seated on a windy hillside in Cornwall, looking out to the sea. My children are behind me at play—you can see them in the background. I wasn't even looking at the camera, and I wasn't in the center of the frame. My hair blew across my face. My husband took it at high noon, and now I see it's a little bleached out, and it is wildly inappropriate for the author's photo, although it reveals a good deal true about me. It says I like to be a small part of a field, that I don't like looking directly at the camera, that a sidelong view is the preferable one, and that my hair tends to be messy. These revelations of character were not what was wanted. My editor sent it back, saying, what we want is a photo about which the potential reader picking up the book will say, *Ah, there's the writer, front and center.*

I didn't know what it meant to identify myself as *the writer front and center.* How does one convey the *identity* of *the writer?* Was I supposed to model myself on an established image of what we think of when we envision a writer? Was I supposed to project an image the photographer understood as fulfilling some idea of what it is to be a writer? Photos of writers emphasize their intelligence, their austerity, and even their intentionality. Some famous ones, like the photos of Auden, show every line of his face, as if genius earned every crease. An image must be generated, produced. My writer self must be tricked to come out and be captured. How can I find a gesture, a pose, an attitude of the head that externalizes the writer in me? It was too much for me because try as I might I didn't have an image of the image I was supposed to project. I didn't and don't know what the writer inside me looks like. I only know her from the inside out, how it feels to be me. I can't pull my insides out for the camera; I can only do that for the page—my page.

I realized that the "author's photograph" is a species of portraiture best understood within the realm of advertising and not art or truth. What my editor wanted was for me to lock down an identity through an image, to self-brand and produce a portrait in the style of Marion Ettlinger, the photographer who has become famous for her author portraits. The list of writers she has photographed is a virtual who's who of American letters. The photographs are stylized, staged in what will become iconic poses that will become synonymous with the subject's writing. Under Ettlinger's gaze Richard Ford's blue eyes become icier, windows onto the soul of his penetrating style. Joyce Carol Oates looks like an aged Catherine up from the grave to knock at the window at the Heights. But these Ettlingers also give the impression of being Photoshopped—skin is luminous, eyes glisten with intensity. There's nothing transient about them or caught on the fly in the mess of living. The underlying message is we shouldn't mistake this person for one of us. Ettlinger burnishes.

We only have one authenticated portrait of Emily Dickinson—a daguerreotype taken at Mount Holyoke in 1847. In it Emily is front and center, the only subject, and stares straight ahead with large doe-brown eyes. Taken when Emily was in her mid-teens, it supplants any image of the writer as an adult that would shape our view of her or alter what our imagination has conferred.

In 1862 Emily replied to Thomas Wentworth Higginson's request that she send a current photo by saying she could only send a verbal portrait. She wrote: "I am small, like the Wren, and my Hair is bold, like a Chestnut Bar—and my eyes, like the Sherry in the Glass, that the Guest leaves." She asked, "Would this do just as well?"

Having given up on my existing photographs, I went to a recommended professional photographer. After shooting fifty photographs, he concluded that I was a difficult subject. He didn't say impossible, but that's what he thought. I couldn't mount an argument against his view, for I had long held the same one. He had me sit on a stool for two hours in a blackened room with various white umbrella-like structures and lights behind me. My face hurt from trying to smile at nothing but myself. I couldn't tuck my chin in, as he advised, turn half way around on the stool's perch, and rest my head on what suddenly struck me as a monstrously large hand, as if straddling thought itself. When he showed me the resultant proofs, they were hideous: I looked older than my mother and twice as miserable.

My last-ditch stab at producing a satisfactory image was to ask a friend, Robert Turney, to take my photo. We went up to the second floor of his house, where he smokes and works without disturbance, and he proceeded to talk to me and snap away. There was some setup, lights were attended to. I was alone, utterly alone. Not a thing to hold onto, to lean against, to put before me. I never forgot that I was posing in front of a lens—still I tried to allow myself to become an object for the photographer to take. In the proofs, I looked more like myself, that is to say, I recognized myself in the photos, which I had not done with the others. The selected photo came about as close as I was going to get in fulfilling my editor's wishes. I am front and center, and my hand is raised against my cheek in a writer's pose. There's a touch of sadness in my face, as there almost always is when I am not enlivened by others. There is simply nothing to be done about that.

It's suitable. I look thoughtful, contemplative as a writer should. Nevertheless, my photo is a pose, a make-believe image of *the* writer. I was instructed to hold my hand up to my face. I don't know exactly what this posture is supposed to portray—writer as thinker? I had done my best to fold myself into the writer's pose, to match myself to it. But I haven't transcended it, which is what I now see I wanted. I wanted to provide what my publisher wanted *and* speak something of myself.

Now when I look at the photo I see how artificial it is, something cooked up between the publisher, the photographer, and me to give the book the image publishers think is required. It is an image of the made-up writer. A truer representation of me as writer would be … what? I'm not sure, since when I most feel the writer in me, I disappear inside the work. I don't know how to make that visible.

It's taken me a long time to see that my image of the writer is the image of my mother when she was young. One photograph spoke to me—it looks like an official photo, perhaps a school photo. My mother is angled to the side, not looking straight ahead; her long neck rises from the V shape of a dark velvet blouse. The background is dark, my mother's hair is dark, swept off her face in waves, her lips are dark. She looks sad and serious and waiting. I don't know what she is waiting for—perhaps for her life to begin.

Where does this leave me? What would I prefer—no photo at all? Should my dust cover have a blank white space? Why not let it be up to the reader to imagine what the writer looks like? Ideally, I'd want a photo where I could say what Patti Smith said about the portrait Robert Mapplethorpe made for her cover of *Horses*: "I had no sense of how it would look, just that it should be true." Maybe it's as simple and as hard as that. The truest photo of me was my senior high school photo in the yearbook of the Moravian Seminary for Girls, in Bethlehem, Pennsylvania.

The morning of the photo my mother had picked me up at my friend's house where I had spent the night. When I got into the car, on the bench seat between us lay a lone red rose my mother had snipped from the bushes beneath her bedroom window. She had wrapped it in a damp paper towel and placed it in a plastic bag to protect its fresh perfection. Now it lay between us on the green front seat of her Monte Carlo, awaiting the moment in which she would present it to me. I was going to hold the rose as I posed for my senior photo.

At the end of our half-hour trip we passed through the elevated wrought-iron gates that marked the entrance to Moravian, and rolled up to the front of Main, the old edifice that housed offices and served as the dormitory for boarders. There my mother dropped me off. As I got out of the car, she picked up the rose, as if lifting her own emotions, and gave it to me. She said nothing more and departed down the curving drive in her green mist Monte Carlo, in a hurry to complete her remaining errands for the day.

If she had glanced back in the rearview mirror, my mother would have seen a slim girl of sixteen in a skirt and blouse of matching fabric, red with white polka dots, a sash at the waist and a ruffle at the hem, holding a red rose inside a plastic bag.

I had given a lot of thought to this photo—what to wear, where to stand, what pose to hold. The choices seemed momentous, for a vision of myself was at stake. This would not be a spontaneous snapshot, raggedly composed and stuffed into a family album to be forgotten. I was creating a picture for posterity, a portrait that would be distributed to friends and relatives. A complicated task had to be accomplished. I had to fashion an image for my future, to create the person I wanted to become, a self-portrait of my dreams. I had to gather the past into the present moment, the click and flash of the camera, and then shatter it with my longing for something more. I wanted to reveal a truth, to find it inside me and show it to others. It would live on in the yearbook as a record of who I was and would be.

My hair was pulled back and pinned sloppily behind my ears, with tendrils falling loose over my eyes. Leaning lightly against a tree trunk, I bent one leg behind the other, looked into the camera, and smiled, ethereal and spindly, like a wobbly fawn who has wandered off from her doe. Sunlight dappled through the branches, and leaves lay adrift on the ground. In my right hand I held my mother's rose at the axis of my body, resting my left hand on the arch of a thick branch. The rose was slightly open on its long and slender stem, like me.

We changed to another pose. Without shoes, I climbed into the cradle of the strong branch on which I had rested my hand. I leaned forward from the foliage, dangling my legs in a secret current, as if balanced against the wind on a strong raft, young yet fragile, a little flushed, a hint of fatigue under my eyes. I looked almost at the camera, a sidelong quick glance, mouth slightly open as if I had something to say but thought better of it or did not have the words.

This was the closest I could come to the truth of a vision of myself.

I didn't imagine that I was immortal, as do some of the young. Some think they're invulnerable, and they thrill to risks because they can't imagine a bad end to their own story. Let the others crash and burn, they say, it won't be me. I did not count myself among these invulnerable ones. I thought I would be felled, and I did the risky thing anyway. I wouldn't say I courted death, that I had a death wish. Neither of these descriptions fit me. I wasn't running toward the end, but I believed death lived inside me. I had an expiration date. I had a case of fatalism so deep I might have been born with it. Mine was a life in which everything inside me would bloom for a time and then die.

All of this was in the yearbook portrait. In my face you could see my mother's gift of a rose, and see innocence left behind. There was yearning, like my mother's yearning, yearning for who knew what—for something more, a new thing, for my life to get started. My eyes were steady, as if I felt no doubts about what I'd embarked on, an expression that said, *Now my life is truly going to begin.* You might see in my face the age behind the innocence, the calm glance of one who thinks she sizes up the world dispassionately.

I looked delicate and easy to break. I would be broken—you could see that in my future. I was dressed in innocence, innocence of the body, of the mind and spirit, not yet aware of the instruments that people make of one another. There was something undecided and insubstantial about me, something that had the power to arouse. I didn't yet know that my vulnerability would compel desire. Whatever gifts I bore, I bore unknowingly. Though I was the picture of young life and girlhood, the moment was elegiac.

There was a sense of something ending in my face. I was my mother's daughter.

Acknowledgments

Material has been adapted from the following publications:

The Art of Being Born	*Hotel Amerika*
Autumn Sonata	*Kenyon Review*
The Blue Dress	*Hotel Amerika*
Bree Daniels	*Hotel Amerika*
Enough	*Florida Review*
Garbo and the Norns	*Northwest Review*
How to Leave a Room	*Brevity*
I, Swimmer	*Gulf Stream*
Inflammable Questions	*Diagram*
The Making of Mothers: Portraits	*Diagram*
Marilyn Monroe's Feet	*Kenyon Review*
The Mother Bed	*Gettysburg Review*
My Mother's Toenails	*Brevity*
Mothers, Writers	*Manifest Station*
Pose	*South Loop Review*
Purse	*Northwest Review*
The Reading	*You* (Welcome Table Press)
The Rejection	*Kenyon Review*
She and I (A Field of Force)	*Under the Sun*
Sidestroke	*Hotel Amerika*
The Stronger One	*Zone 3*
The Structure of Trouble	*Blurring the Boundaries* (University of Nebraska)
Studio of the Voice	*Hypertext*

Winners of the Wandering Aengus Book Award

Marcia Aldrich: Studio of the Voice

Lucy Ferriss: Meditations for a New Century

Steven Harvey: The Beloved Republic

Amanda Hawkins: When I Say the Bones, I Mean the Bones

Christopher Martin: Firmament

Kevin Miller: Vanish

Michael Schmeltzer: Empire of Surrender

Alina Ştefănescu: dôr

Tarn Wilson: In Praise of Inadequate Gifts